The Lord's Prayer

The Lord's Prayer

Confessing the New Covenant

J. WARREN SMITH

CASCADE *Books* • Eugene, Oregon

THE LORD'S PRAYER
Confessing the New Covenant

Cascade Books
An Imprint of Wipf and Stock Publishers
199 W. 8th Ave., Suite 3
Eugene, OR 97401

www.wipfandstock.com

ISBN 13: 978-1-62564-706-1

Cataloguing-in-Publication Data

Smith, J. Warren, 1964–

    The Lord's Prayer : confessing the new covenant / J. Warren Smith.

    xviii + 132 p. ; 23 cm. Includes bibliographical references.

    ISBN 13: 978-1-62564-706-1

    1. Lord's prayer. 2. Lord's prayer—Devotional literature. I. Title.

BV230 .S52 2015

Manufactured in the U.S.A.   03/03/2015

For
the Wainwrights—
Arthur and Betty, Martin and Philip—
whose devotion to Christ and many kindnesses
to me illustrate what it means to live as
the family of God

And Jesus replied, "Who are my mother, and my brothers and my sisters? . . . Whoever does the will of God is my brother, and sister, and mother."

—MARK 3:33, 35

We are all related to each other under one God the Father, all of us who love him and do his will, and we are both fathers to each other when we care for one another and sons when we submit to each other, and above all, brothers, because our one Father is summoning us to take possession of our inheritance by his will and testimony.

—ST. AUGUSTINE, *DE VERA RELIGIONE* 46.89

Contents

Acknowledgments | ix

A Note on Gender and Language | xi

Introduction | xiii

1   A Higher Righteousness: The Context for
    Jesus's Teaching on Prayer (Matt 6:1–18) | 1

2   A Word about Words | 11

3   Claiming God as Father | 20

4   Becoming Children of Jesus's Father | 28

5   Children of Holiness | 37

6   Praying to Our Father | 47

7   Praying for the Kingdom | 55

8   Praying Hopefully | 64

9   Hungry for Bread | 74

10 Restoring the Covenant | 87

11 "That They May Be One": Forgiveness and Reconciliation | 100

12 Confessing Our Vulnerability | 113

Epilogue: A Life of Doxology | 127

Acknowledgments

ALL FAITHFUL THEOLOGY COMES from the Church. It grows out of the shared life of the baptized and seekers alike desiring to grow in the knowledge and love of God. Even theology written or spoken within college and university settings still comes "from the Church" when it is an expression of the theologian's life in the community of believers and is written ultimately for the edification of that community. Whereas scientists have laboratories to work out their hypotheses, academic theologians like me have studies with desks piled with the Scriptures, concordances, and theological treatises, ancient and modern, or seminar rooms filled with eager students. Here we work out our ideas seeking the illumination of the Spirit who brings fresh insight and right understanding into the wonders of God's plan of salvation. Sometimes the Spirit speaks to us through the words of a twelfth-century tome or a nineteenth-century novel or an essay in a modern journal. Other times the Spirit elicits an insight from the provocative question or thoughtful comment of a student. These insights grow out of sustained conversations with fellow believers, and sometimes with nonbelievers. Either way, these ideas become helpful for our scholarship, teaching, and proclamation of the Gospel.

Sometimes, however, we academics are fortunate enough to have those conversations within the setting of a local congregation or parish. This book on the Lord's Prayer began in just such a context. I am grateful to Bain Jones of Christ Church Raleigh, who invited me to give a series of Lenten lectures for their adult education series on the Lord's Prayer in 2011, and to Mary Ann Andres, who invited me to give the same series at Genesis United Methodist Church in January 2012. It was their engaging questions and encouragement that led me to turn the lectures into this book. I presented later versions of these lectures to the pastors of the Juba Diocese of the Episcopal Church of Sudan, arranged by Darriel Harris; to the pastors of the Yei District of the East Africa Annual Conference of the United Methodist Church; and to my home church, Duke Memorial UMC. Their questions lingered in my thoughts and deepened my understanding, reminding me that we are always students together.

Good feedback is invaluable to every author. I am extremely thankful to Rebecca Hymes-Smith of Duke Divinity School; Lou and Melody Peters of Duke Memorial UMC; Zach Heater, whom I got to know at Duke Youth Academy; and Roger Owens and Ginger Thomas, former co-pastors of Duke Memorial, who gave of their time to read, reflect, and offer suggestions on various chapters throughout the process of writing. Their comments helped me give greater clarity to the writing and challenged me to consider a variety of alternate perspectives on this familiar prayer. I appreciate the thoughtful comments surrounding the issues of gender and language offered by dear colleagues and friends, Holly Taylor Coolman of Providence College and Beth Felker Jones of Wheaton College. As one who is deeply moved by the sung as well as the spoken word but who is incapable of singing in tune, I am extremely thankful to be able to draw on the musical gifts of David Arcus of Duke Divinity School and Duke Chapel, who helped me express in musical terms the beauty of various sung versions of the Lord's Prayer. My research assistants, Jennifer Benedict and Amanda Pittman, have been helpful in locating books that were my literary conversation partners for this project. I am thankful to Chase Thompson for the insights and fruitful questions that he raised during our directed reading on prayer. Most of all I am indebted to my wife, Kim, who has read the whole manuscript at least twice, looking for errors and pressing me to be clearer. Her interest in the project and encouragement for its completion mean more than I can express. Lastly, I am grateful to my children, Katherine and Thomas, who without complaint have let me leave them to give these lectures in various churches and who themselves have listened to these lectures as patiently and attentively as can be expected of a ten- and eight-year-old. *Laus et honor Deo super omnia.*

A Note on Gender and Language

IN THIS BOOK ON the Lord's Prayer, I refer to God as "Father" with the corresponding pronouns "he," "his," and "him." I do not call God "Father" out of some belief that God has gender. I take gender to be bodily characteristics manifest in chromosomal, neurological, or anatomical features that distinguish one gender from the other. Since God is spirit and thus is immaterial and incorporeal, God is without gender. Therefore, I do not assume naively that God is "Father" or male in a biological sense. Neither do I refer to God as "Father" out of insensitivity to some readers' tragic associations of "Father" with their own experience of an abusive father. As one who had a wonderful, if at times competitive, relationship with my father, I grieve for those who suffered betrayal in the form of physical or psychological violence or neglect at their father's hands. As a father myself, I can no longer watch *Law and Order: SVU* because of how intensely disturbing I find the images of a father's sexual abuse of his daughter or son. Rather, I refer to God as "Father" in this book because that is how Jesus addressed God, not only in the prayer that is its subject but also throughout the gospels. All language, especially with reference to God, is metaphorical. No single term or collection of terms names God's essence. This does not mean, however, that all terms are equally suitable for speaking about God. As finite creatures, we are immeasurably different than our eternal and infinite Creator. Though made in God's image, the analogies that can be drawn between God and us based upon our experience as creatures are minimal. Therefore, we are dependent upon God's self-revelation in Christ the incarnate Word to disclose the divine heart and mind. We are also dependent upon the language Jesus chose to describe his Father. When Jesus calls God "Father," he is not giving us an analogy by which to think about God. We are not being invited to impose our conceptions of fatherhood or our associations from our relationship with our own fathers on God. That would be to remake God in our image—and a distorted image at that. Rather, in calling God "Father," Jesus is naming *his* unique and eternal relationship with God that allows him to reveal the Father to us. Moreover, and for the purpose of this prayer particularly, in instructing us his disciples to call God "Father," Jesus is revealing the new relationship *we* gain with God through the new covenant. He expresses that relationship in the language that reflects a first-century understanding of the procreative relationship between the male parent and his offspring and of paternal authority. Yet, as his words to Mary and Joseph after they discovered him in the temple suggest, Jesus did not think that the authority proper to our heavenly Father was transferable to earthly fathers simply because they have the same familial title. In revealing God as our Father, Jesus does disclose the ideal father. To all who have been abused by their earthly father, Jesus says, "Let me show you what fathers should be. Let me show you how fathers should treat their sons and daughters." Until, God forbid, asexual procreation is possible through human cloning, there will continue to be fathers. Instead of abandoning the language, it must be sanctified. We must see beyond our associations with profoundly flawed fathers to the ideal of fatherly love that Jesus calls us to imitate.

When speaking of people I alternate between the generic terms "man," "humanity," and "people" with the alternating pronouns, "he," "she," "his," "her," "him." My reason is grounded in my understanding of the Incarnation. Christ the Word became flesh. He took a particular form of flesh, namely that of a man, a male. Yet, in becoming a male he did not exclude anything essential from that common humanity men, women, and hermaphrodites share. Thus in matters spiritual, there is nothing in either gender that is exclusive of the other; both bear the image of God, in whom there is no gender. Even as we should be able to see ourselves fully represented in Jesus' flesh even if we are not a Middle Eastern Jewish man, so too men and women should hear themselves fully represented in the gendered language of our day.

Introduction

IN OUR MEDIA-DRIVEN SOCIETY it is easy to feel bombarded by words—words that seem to make little difference in our world. Even as Christians we can find ourselves being dismissive of God-talk. Cynically, we say, "I'd rather see a sermon than hear one." Indeed, the words of worship can become so familiar that we find ourselves repeating them without thinking about their meaning. At times, our worship feels stale and repetitious. It is not a conflict between a religion of the head and a religion of the heart. For neither head nor heart is engaged. Our worship can be mere habit, unthinking reflex. Arguably, never is that more true than when we say the Lord's Prayer. Yet this need not be the case.

My life changed significantly in 1974. Before then, my life was that of a United Methodist pastor's son. Ours was a large suburban congregation on the south side of Atlanta within throwing distance of Hartsfield Airport. The people were exceedingly gracious to my family and me. They raised me as their own, encouraging and supporting me right up through my seminary years. But the church was about as "white-bread" as you would imagine, and its worship was just as staid and formal. In the middle of fourth grade, however, I discovered that there were other ways to worship God. In that year my father became a full-time professor of church history at the Interdenominational Theological Center (ITC), an historically black seminary that, together with Clark, Morehouse, Spellman, and others colleges, made up Atlanta University. For the first time in years my father had no standing Sunday morning obligation. He decided to use this freedom to visit the black congregations of Atlanta where his colleagues and students worshipped. This would allow him to be more connected with Atlanta's black community. Often on Sunday mornings my mother and I would tag along.

On these forays to black churches, I discovered two things. First, the services were twice the length but felt half as long as the white services I had known up to that point. The second thing I discovered—or better, rediscovered—was the Lord's Prayer. The energy of worship in those churches was an awakening experience for me. Its spontaneity was refreshing for a ten-year-old boy accustomed to the formal ritual of my home church. One of the churches we attended was old Central United Methodist Church, which was situated between the campuses of Morris Brown and Clark colleges and the office buildings of downtown Atlanta. Under the pastorate of civil rights leader Joseph Lowery, the congregation summed up its ministry with the words "A church at the heart of the city with the city at heart."

There, as at my home church, the pastoral prayer came somewhere in the middle of the service, before the offering; but this prayer was different. Far from being ethereal, the prayer named the needs of his people and the grief of their community. The content of his prayer was down to earth and openly political. But at the close of the prayer the organ began playing and the choir led the congregation into a slow, rhythmic singing of the Lord's Prayer. The only time I had ever heard the Lord's Prayer sung in my church was as an anthem by a visiting black soloist. But as the worshipers of Central United Methodist swayed in their pews and joined their voices with those of the choir, I discovered that the Lord's Prayer could be a time of meditation. Not a prayer to be rushed through to get to the next element of the service, but a time to let one's mind rest in the words that hung in the air. Singing the Lord's Prayer at one-third the speed with which we would have recited it gave me a chance to think about the words I was saying and let my thoughts linger on their meaning. This congregational prayer raised my mind into the presence of God, and I felt no desire to pass quickly from his presence. The sung words of the Lord's Prayer connected the material hurts and spiritual hunger of that congregation with the promise that the Spirit of God was in our midst. The words were no longer rote ritual. They mediated the presence of God.

It is for precisely this reason that words are indispensible to the Christian life: they mediate the reality of Immanuel, God-with-us. The Christian narrative of history begins with the declaration "In the beginning was the *Word*." By the power of his Word, God called creation into being. In the soul-seizing inspiration of the Spirit, the prophets announced the Word of the Lord. And in the fullness of time, the Word became flesh and bone, Jesus of Nazareth, the Messiah. The Word is our Lord. For us, there is often a regrettable disconnect between our words and our actions. For Jesus, the divine Word fully united to a human soul and body, there is no disconnect.

In him, Divine Word and human action were one. Jesus walked the talk of God. So for Jesus, prayer is not merely words. It is a way of life, a way of being in the world, a way of being in relationship with our heavenly Father. Prayer is *how* we walk in the world. Praying the Lord's Prayer is not simply one among many Christian practices; it defines all other practices. It is how we continue to walk with the risen Christ, who is genuinely present with us at the same time that he has ascended to the right hand of the Father. It is our way of being *with* God in our walk.

Even as Christ, the Incarnate Word, was the perfect union of speech and deed, so too must we strive to integrate our words and actions. The prayer-formed life that imitates Christ's life unites the talk of prayer and the walk of prayer. The talk of prayer is our confession of faith, the words with which we name the God in whom we believe and on whom our life is centered. The walk of prayer is how we live into the relationship with this God whom we confess. To put it another way, the words of prayer turn the mind from the mundane distractions that occupy our time and energies and allow us to enter God's presence, listening for God's voice and raising our words of praise and petition. Prayer as a walk or way of life involves practicing the presence of God at all times. It is practicing being God's presence in the world. This is the potential power of the Lord's Prayer. The words of the Lord's Prayer allowed the people of Central Methodist to enter the presence of God so that they could bear the heart of God to the heart of inner-city Atlanta.

The purpose of this book is twofold. First, it is a call to the Church to be active when praying the Lord's Prayer. This call is an invitation to re-imagine the prayer as a confession of the Christian faith—a confession that grounds our lives in the new covenant that Jesus inaugurated at the Last Supper. For this covenant expresses our relationship with the triune God whom we confess to be Lord. Second, it is a guide for our meditation on the words of the Prayer. Jesus's brilliance is evident in how much he packs into a mere three dozen words. A friend, upon hearing that I was writing a book on the Lord's Prayer, remarked, "How can you write a whole book on that? I mean, it's not very long." True, but each phrase is pregnant with meaning, inviting us to linger on and contemplate each petition. I hope that as we reflect on the depth of meaning conveyed in the prayer's pithy phrases, we will come to a more profound understanding of the covenantal relation be-tween us and the God we call "our Father." Out of a deeper understanding of the Lord's Prayer, our own prayers may become more profound and our lives more profoundly grounded in the new covenant we confess.

I said above that this book is intended to help us meditate upon the prayer's meanings (plural), not its meaning (singular). While I am sure that there are some interpretations that are wrong, I am even more confident that the simple phrases of the prayer contain not one meaning but a wealth of meanings. So rich and suggestive are Jesus's brief words that one can discover new meanings in the prayer throughout the course of a long and spiritually reflective life. The best way to recognize the range of meanings implicit in the prayer is to attune one's ear to the way it echoes themes from the whole of the salvation story. I am writing as a theologian whose task is to understand the prayer's possible meanings for the Church within the larger Christian message contained in the whole of sacred Scripture and the Christian tradition. Therefore, I frequently interpret certain expressions in the prayer in the light of the Gospel according to John or the epistles of St. Paul, especially Romans and 1 Corinthians.

Second, like my father—and because of my father's love of church history—I am a church historian. I teach all periods in the Church's past, but my primary area of study is the early Church, the Patristic era that stretches from the death of the apostles through the sixth century. Believing that the Church is best served when each person plays to his or her own strengths, I draw upon what I know best to unpack the nuances of Jesus's words. So I will often incorporate illustrations from early Christian pastors and teachers who commented on the Lord's Prayer.

Why, some may ask, should the Church of the twenty-first century in all its diversity care what dead white guys from the second or fourth centuries said about the Lord's Prayer? First, it is not quite fair to characterize all the fathers as "dead white guys." While they are certainly dead, many of the leading theologians of the early Church were not white or European but African, coming from Egypt or Tunis, or Asian, coming from modern-day Turkey. They are worth listening to for a simple reason: they are among the most profound preachers and insightful theologians the Church has ever known. Even if they are not household names, they are known by pastors and theologians. Often their ideas are foundational for contemporary theology. After all, they are the ones who set the canon of the Old and New Testaments.

To be sure, we modern people have many advantages over our foremothers and fathers of late antiquity. Science has allowed us to develop technologies that let us see further into the vastness of space and deeper into the workings of the atom than our predecessors. But no technological discovery has given us an advantage in seeing into the heart of God, for God is not a material creature that can be examined under a microscope. God is spirit and so can be known only through his working in history, specifically the history of Israel, the life of Jesus, and the expansion of the Church in the first century. God's Spirit did not stop inspiring men and women when the last of the apostles died. The history of the Church is the history of the Spirit's ongoing inspiration of the Church's leaders as they seek to discern the meaning of God's self-revelation in Jesus of Nazareth. So, we have every bit as much to learn from the inspired insights of Origen and Augustine as we do from the most faithful and brilliant commentators of our own age. If St. Paul's metaphor of the body describes the Church across the centuries, then we modern Christians cannot be the proverbial eye who presumptuously says to the hand of the ancient Church "I have no need of you." I hope that this book will introduce you to some of these ancient and venerable figures and that their insights will deepen your insight as you pray and live into the Lord's Prayer.

1

A Higher Righteousness: The Context for Jesus's Teaching on Prayer (Matt 6:1–18)

"Beware of practicing your piety before men ..."

WHEN WE THINK ABOUT the "Lord's Prayer," we think chiefly of the words Jesus instructed his disciples to say. In fact, however, the Lord's Prayer as a model for Christian prayer rightly includes Jesus's full instruction on prayer in the Sermon on the Mount (Matt 6:9–13) and the parallel account in the Sermon on the Plain (Luke 11:2–4). Jesus's teaching can be broken into two parts: the "how" of prayer and the "what" of prayer. The "how" of prayer is the proper manner of prayer. The "what" of prayer refers to its structure and substance. Jesus's discussion of prayer comes in a section of the sermon devoted to the subject of works of piety such as fasting, praying, and giving alms to the poor. He introduces this topic with a stern warning: "Beware of practicing your piety [*dikaiosynēn*] before men in order to be seen by them; for then you will have no reward from your Father who is in heaven" (Matt 6:1 RSV). The word in the Greek manuscripts of the New Testament that is translated "piety" in the RSV is *dikaiosynē*. The more common translation of *dikaiosynē* is "righteousness," meaning to be in right relationship with God. It describes a holy life devoted to God. Therefore, Jesus's warning could just as well be translated thus: "Beware of performing works of righteousness ..." Translating *dikaiosynē* as "righteousness" instead of "piety" is helpful because it allows us to see the important connection between Jesus's discussion of prayer in Matt 6:1–18 and his teachings on Moses and the Pharisees earlier in Matt 5:17–20.

The Righteousness of Hypocrites

In Matthew's Gospel, Jesus is presented as the new Moses. Even as Moses went up Mt. Sinai to receive the law, so Jesus delivered his teachings on a mountaintop. Moreover, when Jesus commented on the law of Moses, he followed the formula "You have heard it said of old [i.e., in the law of Moses], but I say to you . . ." Then Jesus expands Moses's commandments with his own teachings. Although Matthew presents Jesus as the new law-giver, he is clear that Jesus came not to overturn the law of Moses. So Jesus explains his intention in these teachings:

> Think not that I have come to abolish the law and the prophets; I have come not to abolish them but to fulfill them. For truly, I say to you, till heaven and earth pass away, not an iota, not a dot, will pass from the law until all is accomplished. Whoever then relaxes one of the least of these commandments and teaches men so, shall be called least in the kingdom of heaven; but he who does them and teaches them shall be called great in the kingdom of heaven. For I tell you, unless your righteousness [*dikaiosynē*] exceeds that of the scribes and Pharisees, you will never enter the kingdom of heaven. (Matt 5:17–20)

The law was given to Moses on Sinai in order to train Israel how to live righteously. Far from doing away with the law, Jesus has come to bring the law to its fullness or completion. As great a prophet as Moses was, Jesus is even greater. He is the Christ, the Son of the living God. His teachings in the Sermon on the Mount raise the bar. He reveals the perfect righteousness God desires and expects of his people. Since Jesus is greater than Moses, Jesus's disciples are held to a higher standard of righteousness (*dikaiosynē*) than Moses's disciples (the scribes and Pharisees). Therefore, in Matt 6:1–18 Jesus teaches his disciples what they must do in order for their righteousness to exceed that of the scribes and Pharisees.

At the heart of Jesus's criticism of the scribes and Pharisees is that they make a public display of righteousness in the manner of hypocrites (*hypokritai*). Instead, Jesus says, his disciples should practice their fasting, praying, and almsgiving in secret. Why is Jesus so insistent that works of righteousness be done in secret? Why is performing works of righteousness before men an act of hypocrisy? To us, hypocrisy means saying one thing publicly but doing another thing privately. The person who publicly gives alms to the poor is not necessarily being duplicitous or trying to deceive people. Moreover, Jesus's insistence that works of righteousness not be done before men seems to contradict what he says earlier in the Sermon on the Mount:

> You are the light of the world. A city set on a hill cannot be hid.
> Nor do men light a lamp and put it under a bushel, but on a stand,
> and it gives light to all in the house. Let your light so shine *before*
> *men*, so that they may *see your good works* and give glory to your
> Father who is in heaven. (Matt 5:14–16)

If God made us the light of the world, then our good works should be done publicly so that they may be seen. If works of righteousness are done in secret, who but God will know? How will people be drawn to God unless they see God's goodness in our good works? How can they believe the faith we proclaim unless they also see that we put our money where our mouth is, that we walk the talk? How can our lives be a witness to the goodness of God and bring God glory unless others see our good works?

The hypocrisy of the scribes and Pharisees takes many forms. But their greatest hypocrisy is that they set themselves up as examples of righteousness while they strive for personal glory rather than the glory of God. As Jesus said, they loved to be seen by people so that they would be admired and honored by them. They gave to the poor in ostentatious ways that got them noticed. When they fasted they wore dour expressions on their faces so that people would see how hard their fasting was. They prayed in the most conspicuous places so that people could not help noticing them. Yet in seeking the favor of people rather than God, they had missed the very goal of righteousness. For the aim of all holiness is to be pleasing to God. When the Scottish Olympian Eric Liddell, whose victory in the 1924 Olympic games was immortalized in the movie *Chariots of Fire*, explained his love of running, he said, "God made me fast; and when I run, I feel his pleasure." That is true righteousness. It is a desire that God may be glorified in seeing his will fulfilled in us. The scribes and the Pharisees loved the praise of men more than God's pleasure. So they cultivated the appearance of righteousness that they might gain glory for themselves rather than for God. The irony is that because their adherence to the law was motivated by a desire for personal glory rather than a love for God, they failed to fulfill true righteousness.

By acting in order to gain the approval of men, the scribes and Pharisees failed to fulfill true righteousness in another way. They failed to embody the *humility* necessary for true righteousness. The truly righteous person realizes that her righteousness is not, properly speaking, *her* work, but the work of God in her. One of the most brilliant teachers of the early Church, an Egyptian named Origen, said that we are called to shine light in a dark world just as the moon gives light at night. The brightness of the moon is not the moon's own light; it is merely the reflection of the greater light of the sun. So, too, our good works are not our own but the work of God's grace in us. God is their true source. The person whose life is centered upon God knows this. She realizes that her righteousness is but a reflection of God's perfect goodness. We are the light of the world when, in our good works, the world sees the goodness of God and so is drawn to worship and follow him. Humility is not the denial of the goodness of our good works. It simply desires that our good works point beyond ourselves to the One who alone is good, the true object of our glory and praise. Humble Christians are like friends at a wedding who do not upstage the bride and bridegroom, but are content to step to the side and allow them to have their day. We say with John the Baptist, "[Christ] must increase, but I must decrease" (John 3:30). Unlike the scribes and Pharisees who enjoyed basking in society's acclaim and recognition, Jesus's humble disciples shy away from the spotlight. They prefer to recede into the shadows, that God may occupy the foreground of people's thoughts. When God takes center stage to receive the crowd's ovation, then true righteousness finds its delight.

Secret Righteousness

So the humility of righteousness desires that God, not man, receive glory. But that still does not answer the question, why perform works of righteousness *in secret*? After all, Jesus could just as easily have told the disciples, "When you fast, pray, and give alms, do not seek the praise of men, but that of God alone." Surely that would have been consistent with his earlier command, "Let your good works be seen by men . . ." Why does he command instead that they be done in secret? As with most of Jesus's teachings, there is no one simple answer. But let me suggest two possibilities.

First, we never know our *real* motive for doing anything. Our ego or vanity or pride insinuates itself into the situation. We never know whether we are acting primarily out of love for God or out of self-interest. T. S. Eliot's play *Murder in the Cathedral* tells the story of the conflict between the English king Henry II and the archbishop of Canterbury, Thomas Becket. In an attempt to gain control of the Church in England, King Henry appointed his friend, Becket, to the position of archbishop. The king soon discovered that Becket would not be a pawn acting in the interests of the crown. Instead, Becket became a defender of the Church's rights and prerogatives. When Henry trespassed on those rights, Becket opposed him and was forced into exile. After lengthy negotiations, Becket was allowed to return to Canterbury. But the tension remained. Becket would not submit to all the king's demands. As the scene for another clash between king and archbishop is set, Becket, like Jesus in the wilderness, encounters three tempters. The first tempter invites him to be reconciled to the king, renew their friendship, and keep the peace. The second counsels him to resign as archbishop and take back real power as the king's chancellor and chief minister who sets and carries out the king's policies. The third tempter recommends that Becket form a political alliance with the barons, who are the king's rivals, to overthrow Henry. All these temptations Becket summarily dismisses. But then a fourth, unexpected tempter comes offering him the glory of martyrdom:

> When king is dead, there's another king,
> And one more king is another reign.
> King is forgotten, when another shall come:
> Saint and Martyr rule from the tomb.
> Think, Thomas, think of enemies dismayed,
> Creeping in penance, frightened of a shade;
> Think of pilgrims, standing in line
> Before the glittering jeweled shrine,
> From generation to generation
> Bending the knee in supplication,
> Think of miracles by God's grace,
> And think of your enemies, in another place . . .
> Seek the way of martyrdom, make yourself the lowest
> On earth, to be high in heaven.

This was Becket's blind spot. Becket loved his own virtue—and the honor and esteem that was its reward. By opposing the king and being martyred as a champion of the Church, Becket would gain the fame, praise, and prayers of Englishmen for centuries, until Christ returns to separate the sheep from the goats. Then Saint Thomas Becket would stand in judgment over his enemies, sentencing them to perdition. With the coming of the fourth tempter, Becket confronts his own confused motives. Is his willingness to die defending the Church's rights an act of self-emptying obedience to God? Or is it the exact opposite—not an act of self-denial and humble service but one of self-aggrandizement intended to bring him fame and glory? If he dies seeking his own glory rather than God's, even if his cause is just, then he will have sinned before God. "The last temptation is the greatest treason: To do the right deed for the wrong reason." Which is his real motive? He cannot know for sure. Nor can we be sure of our motives. Rarely are we absolutely certain whether our acts of righteousness and charity are done chiefly for God's glory or for our own.

What is the solution to this conundrum? Jesus gives us the answer: "Perform your works of righteousness in secret." When we give to the poor anonymously, or fast without telling anyone, or pray in the solitude of our bedroom with the door closed, then we give up all possibility of others knowing about our deeds. Then the poor who do not know the name of those who gave money to pay the month's rent will be grateful to God and give him the glory. Acting in anonymity we perform a sacrifice; we sacrifice the recognition of men. It is our way of saying to God, "I am content with your judgment. All I desire is that you find pleasure in my work." This secrecy is the humility of true righteousness.

To be sure, even when we do good works in secret, there is the danger that our motives may be questionable. We may give in order to feel good about ourselves or to assuage middle-class guilt. It is also possible that we are motivated by a sense of *noblesse oblige*, that sense of duty to those we see as "beneath us." Yet, when we give out of love—love for God and genuine love for our neighbor—our works of charity produce not a feeling of self-satisfaction so much as a feeling of inadequacy. We realize how much greater the need of our neighbor is than our ability to provide for her. When we act out of love, rather than a sense of class obligation, there is no room for pride. Once again, righteous love is more concerned for the needs and feelings of others than for making us feel better.

The second potential reason Jesus tells his followers to practice their righteousness in secret is that secrecy is a mark of our *intimacy* with God. The highest goal of the Christian life is friendship with God. As Jesus told his disciples, "I no longer call you servants but friends" (John 15:15). As friends, the Christian's experience of intimate communion with God is a reward in itself. Paul describes this intimacy when he says of our face-to-face encounter with God at the resurrection, "Now I know in part, then I shall understand fully, even as I have been fully known" (1 Cor 13:12). What greater pleasure is there than being in the company of that friend who knows us inside and out and desires our flourishing? Perhaps the closest analogy to spiritual intimacy with God is the intimacy between husband and wife. Indeed, Jesus, following the Song of Songs, compares his relationship with his disciples to that of a bridegroom and his bride. Simply being alone together and enjoying each other's company, united emotionally and physically, distinguishes the friendship of marriage from all other friendships. The secrecy of this intimacy defines the uniqueness of that relationship. Take away the secrecy and the intimacy is compromised. To "kiss and tell" would be to debase the relationship. It would betray the distinctive confidence that husband and wife share in that moment of vulnerability when they open themselves up and give themselves over in trust to their beloved.

The exhibitionism of the scribes and Pharisees, their public display, has a parallel in the exhibitionism of Curley, a character in John Steinbeck's novella *Of Mice and Men*, which is set on a ranch in California during the Great Depression. The ranch is almost exclusively a world of men. The lone female is a pretty but lonely young woman who is married to Curley, the boss's son. Highly conscious of being short, Curley tries to prove his manliness by picking fights with bigger fellows, who wisely back down lest they get fired by Curley's father. Curley also lords over the other men that he is the only one who has a pretty young wife waiting for him at the end of the day. To make his point, he always wears a glove on one hand. He brags to the men that he covers this hand in Vaseline to keep it smooth for his wife. Curley leaves it to the men's imagination what he does with this smooth hand. The gloved hand is a sign of his sexual prowess and his pretty wife is a symbol of his manliness. Curley puts his intimacy with his wife on display to prove to the ranch hands that he is every bit as much a man as they are. In so doing, he violates the spirit of the relationship wives and husbands enjoy. Gone is the trust and security of the marriage bed.

A lawyer once told me that unless the confidentiality of the attorney-client privilege is sacrosanct there is no trust and the relationship is broken. Likewise, when secrecy in marriage is given up, so is the privilege of intimacy. For without the trust of secrecy, we forfeit the blessed freedom of being open and fully honest about our aspirations and our proudest accomplishments, our deepest fears and vulnerabilities. The scribes and Pharisees are guilty of the same sort of exhibitionism as Curley. To turn our works of righteousness into opportunities for gaining public approval is to debase our relationship with God. It makes friendship with God not an end in itself but a means of making ourselves look good.

Private prayer is a time of intimacy between God and his children. As we shall see, prayer is never a wholly private matter. We always pray as members of the community of faith, the family of God. Prayer always will be an essential component of our public, corporate worship. But prayer as a part of the daily rhythms of our life is far more often a private affair. How often do the gospel writers tell of Jesus's withdrawing from the disciples and going to a lonely place to pray? Or of his sending his followers across the Sea of Galilee that he might pray alone? So when Jesus commands his disciples to go into their room and close the door that they may pray in secret, he is inviting them to enter into the very intimacy with the Father that he enjoys. For in the privacy of our bedroom or study or under a favorite tree by the lake, we are free to turn our minds completely to God and bare our souls to him. In the seclusion of prayer, we seek to minimize mundane distractions in order to center our thoughts upon God and listen for the word spoken by his Spirit. In the secret intimacy of prayer, we speak the fears and anxieties that we would share with no one else. There and then we find the privilege of speaking with the One who, as the psalmist says, has searched me and known me and knows altogether every word before it is on my tongue. Before the God who knows us completely—warts and all—and still loves us, there is the freedom to be honest and open in the security of his love that there is with no one else.

Training in Secret

To be sure, not all righteous works can be kept secret. Serving in a soup kitchen, giving a testimonial on stewardship Sunday about the value of tithing, leading in the pastoral prayer—all of these are good and righteous deeds. They are by their very nature public. They are the way we let our light shine before people as a witness to God's goodness. Are such conspicuous works a violation of Jesus's warning against practicing our righteousness in public? No. They are simply how one lives a righteous life as a social animal. We do not live in the solitude of a desert isle. We live in community. Our piety cannot be kept entirely secret, completely hidden from public notice. The Christian life is unavoidably lived out in the public square. Our understanding of

Christ's call "Come and follow me" is determinative, implicitly or explicitly, of all we do, anywhere and everywhere, in public or in private.

So how do we reconcile Jesus's declaration that we are the light of the world whose good works are seen by others (Matt 5) with his warning not to practice our righteousness in order to been seen (Matt 6)? Practicing the righteousness of praying, fasting, and almsgiving in secret trains us to conform our lives to that form of righteousness common to all godly work. For when, especially during Lent, we concentrate upon praying, fasting, and giving alms secretly, we learn the spiritual pleasure of intimacy with God. Like Jesus withdrawing from the disciples to pray to his heavenly Father, we discover the blessing of being alone with God, of opening our hearts to the one who knows our hearts through and through. We also find satisfaction in doing what is pleasing to God and delighting solely in his pleasure. When we can be content with God's approval and when we are eager for the stillness and solitude of God's companionship in prayer, we become less concerned about what others think of us. We grow indifferent to people's fickle praise. Our sense of self does not rest upon the approval of others.

To be sure, we must always be open to the advice and even rebuke of our brothers and sisters, for we do not have an objective view of ourselves. The loving judgment of a sister in the faith is constructive criticism that is invaluable if we are to grow in holiness. At the same time, we should take seriously the compliments people give us. I remember going up to a professor to tell him how much I appreciated his lecture. Perhaps trying to be humble, he barely acknowledged the compliment. Whatever his intention, he came off as arrogant, indifferent to my reaction to his lecture. I felt rather small, unworthy of his notice. Every pastor has stood in the receiving line as people file by on their way out of the church. When we are young in the ministry, we are eager for compliments, for our people's adulation and approval. Eventually, we mature in the ministry. We realize that God may use our words to touch people in different ways. We are thankful for those times when our words have struck a chord with our people collectively or even with just a few individuals. But we also learn not to place too much trust in a pat comment such as "Nice job" or "Good sermon." Praise alone cannot sustain our ministry. If our sense of self and of our ministry becomes dependent on the compliments of our people, we as pastors are bound to be miserable. Human accolades are neither lasting nor are they a good measure of our faithfulness. As Jesus cautioned his disciples, "Woe to you, when all men speak well of you, for so their fathers did to the false prophets" (Luke 6:26). Instead, we learn to trust the judgment of our own conscience as to how worthy an offering to God our sermon was. This is true not just of preachers and their sermons but of all works of righteousness, those of laity and clergy alike. For learning to be content with God's true but gracious judgment is the mark of spiritual maturity. It is a maturity that exceeds that of the scribes and Pharisees, for it is the maturity of genuine righteousness.

Although we often pray the Lord's Prayer in the context of public worship, we have missed the mark of true righteousness if we care what others think about us when they see and hear us pray. If, moreover, we make the Lord's Prayer a feature only of our public worship, we miss out on the blessings of spiritual intimacy. As we shall discover in the following chapters, each clause of the prayer is pregnant with meaning. If we take time to meditate on a particular clause, rather than racing through the prayer at our normal speed, then we may hear our Father speak to us through his Spirit. When our spirit communes with his Spirit, we experience intimacy with God. For in the intimacy of prayer the Spirit opens to us a deeper knowledge of the Father's love. Then the God who, as the psalmist says, "formed us in secret" in our mother's womb may reform us in his image in the secret, inner space of prayer.

2

A Word about Words

When trying to help a person make the first step to God in prayer, a pastor might tell her, "Just say what is in your heart." That is good advice. The first step in going from thinking of God as an idea to experiencing God as a companion and friend is to get accustomed to speaking to the One whose invisible presence cannot be detected with the senses. At first, we feel self-conscious and more than a little foolish. It is as if we are just talking to the air. The only way to overcome that initial awkwardness is to break the silence and reach out with our words, however feeble they seem. Indeed, what God desires most is that we call upon him. This is the first act of faith. It is our act of will, our choosing to respond to God who has been making his presence known to us. In ways subtle—sometimes perceptible only in retrospect—or conspicuous, God has been saying, "I am the One who made you. You need me. Come to me." And with our first awkward words, we come.

But when we try to make a regular practice of prayer, we quickly discover that "just saying what is in our heart" is neither easy nor satisfying. Our once spontaneous prayer sounds like rehearsed speech. Our prayer feels stale. We've run out of new things to say to God, so we repeat the same phrases from the day before and the day before that. The words do not express what is on our heart. Instead of being an enriching conversation with our beloved, prayer becomes awkward, no more enriching than polite small talk. This new spiritual relationship, like a passionless marriage, is already in a rut.

Pretentious Babble

Jesus knew that his disciples faced this problem. It is precisely this experience that caused the disciples to say, "Teach us to pray" (Luke 11:1). Because we often fumble for the right words in prayer, Jesus gave us words with which to focus our attention on God and so let our mind enter his presence. But before giving us the words that we call the Lord's Prayer or the Our Father, Jesus needed to say a few words about words—specifically, about the sorts of words that we should avoid.

"When you pray, do not heap up empty phrases [*battalogēsēte*] as the Gentiles do; for they think that they will be heard for their many words" (Matt 6:7). What are the "empty phrases" characteristic of pagan prayers? The Greek word that the RSV translates "heap up empty phrases" is a form of the verb *battologeō*. It is a compound word: *battos*, meaning "babble," and *logos*, meaning "word" or "speech." So *battologeō* carries the sense of "babble" or "vain repetition," as when a small child says a new word over and over again because he likes the sound of it. Among adults, *battologeō* may characterize the writing style of college sophomores who pile one fifty-cent word on top of another so that they will sound sophisticated and intellectual. In a small child it is cute or amusing; in a college student it simply sounds pretentious. Yet here, as in most studies of Scripture, the meaning of Jesus's words is deeper than the meaning we gain simply by studying the etymology of the Hebrew or Greek terms.

As any good preacher does, Jesus employs the familiar language of Scripture to deliver his message. Here he reminded his disciples of an insight found in one of the books of Wisdom literature, Ecclesiastes. With its relentless refrain "Vanity of vanities, all is vanity," Ecclesiastes pours ice water on our daydreams and delusions of grandeur. A people whose lives are as fleeting as the fading flower cannot presume to grasp the wisdom of their Creator. Our words cannot express the inscrutable judgments of God. Therefore, Ecclesiastes warns us, "Guard your steps when you go to the house of God; to draw near to listen is better than to offer the sacrifice of fools; for they do not know that they are doing evil. Be not rash with your mouth, nor let your heart be hasty to utter a word before God, for God is in heaven, and you upon earth; therefore let your words be few" (Eccl 5:1–2).

The house of God is the temple that the Psalms describe as a house of prayer and worship. What is the proper disposition for worship? It is the posture of humble submission, of the servant who does not presume to address his master but waits for his master to speak. When you enter the temple, Ecclesiastes commends, don't be quick to speak, but be silent that you may listen for your Master's word. Nor should you come to the temple thinking that your words will impress and move God to do your bidding, as if God were like people at a political rally whom the politician hopes to persuade with his winning words. *God is in heaven*; he transcends space and time. The span of the universe he envelops within his being. By contrast, we mortals occupy a single place on a small planet alone in the vastness of space. To such a God, our many big words are but a small and unimpressive thing. So, Ecclesiastes counsels, a few carefully chosen words that respond to God's word are preferable to many empty words spoken only to sound impressive. God is impressed only by true humility—a humility manifest in the few simple words we pray in the Lord's Prayer.

Empty Petitions

The babble of "empty phrases" against which Jesus warns may not refer to the words themselves, but rather to the content of our petition. In Origen's sermons on the Lord's Prayer, he observed that we know neither how to pray nor for what to pray. The "empty phrases" Jesus has in mind, he suggested, are our petitions for things that are of no spiritual importance. Often our prayers resemble laundry lists of trivial, bothersome tasks—if only God would deliver us from them or make them easier! Such prayers assume that God is our servant whose job is to take care of the mundane unpleasantness of life that annoys us.

Even worse, Origen said, often we pray to be delivered from the very things that we need to grow spiritually. How often do we pray to be delivered from adversity and hardship? As a parent, the petition "keep them safe" is an automatic one. Christianity is not a masochistic religion. We do not seek out adversity, nor should we. In the first centuries of the early Church, some Christians, desiring to imitate Christ's passion and death, actually handed themselves over to the Roman authorities in hopes of being martyred. This practice the Church condemned as contrary to the gospel; Jesus did not hand himself over to Pilate but waited to be arrested. We do not need to go looking for hardship and suffering; they will find us soon enough. But, Origen said, God often uses our sufferings to train or discipline us in the way of discipleship.

Paul, in Romans 5, declares the good news that through Christ we have the hope of sharing in the glory of God. Yet that hope will become reality at Christ's return only if we have persevered in the faith. Perseverance, however, comes only with discipline and practice. Therefore, Paul declares, "we rejoice in our suffering, knowing that suffering produces endurance, and endurance produces character, and character produces hope, and hope does not disappoint us" (Rom 5:4–5). A marathon runner builds up the endurance necessary to complete all twenty-six miles by conditioning her body and mind to withstand the pain and will-breaking fatigue of the final ten miles. So too the Christian rejoices in the midst of her suffering, Paul says, knowing that the suffering is training her to endure by cleaving to God and seeking his sustaining grace.

The Southern writer Flannery O'Connor suffered from lupus, a painful disease that causes the body to produce antibodies that attack its own tissues and affects the blood, joints, and internal organs. Her father died of lupus when she was fifteen. From age twenty on, painful bouts of lupus kept her a prisoner in her own home; the disease claimed her life at age thirty-nine. Toward the end of her life, O'Connor wrote, "I feel sorry for those who do not experience a period of suffering before they die; for they sure miss one of God's tender mercies." These words can come only from one who has suffered greatly. Were they from anyone else they would not have the ring of authenticity but the unreality of exaggerated piety. O'Connor recognized that when we are in robust health we take life for granted; we become forgetful of our mortality. We become complacent and fail to see our need to cleave to the One who is the source of life. During an illness, we experience our brokenness and are confronted with the reality of our own mortality. Then we realize our dependence upon God to sustain us and ultimately to deliver us from death. If God uses adversity and suffering to break us of our spiritual complacency and turn us back to him, then instead of praying for a life free of such hardships—such petitions are foolish and vain anyway—we should pray for the grace that is greater than our own strength, the grace to sustain us in our adversity.

Prayers to an Omniscient God?

Whether the "empty phrases" or "babble" of the Gentiles' prayers refer to long, verbose prayers, trivial prayers, or prayers that seek worldly rather than spiritual goods, Jesus himself tells us why all such prayers are foolish. "Do not be like the Gentiles, for your Father knows what you need *before* you ask him" (Mat 6:8). The Gentiles whom Jesus has in mind were non-Jews of the Mediterranean world. In each province of the Roman Empire, there were temples dedicated to the local deities as well as temples erected by the Roman legions and dedicated to the gods of the Roman pantheon, such as Jupiter and Juno, Minerva and Apollo. These gods were not transcendent spiritual beings but were essentially superhuman beings with tremendous power. They also suffered from human vices: vanity, jealousy, lust, irascibility. Therefore, the purpose of sacrifices and elaborate prayers was to get their attention and earn their favor. With long prayers cluttered with lofty words, pagan priests sought to appeal to the vanity of the gods. If the particular god was satisfied with the priest's piety demonstrated in his words and sacrifices, then the god would grant the petition.

The God of Israel is no mere superhuman figure. As the One who is called "the great I Am," he is the transcendent God who is Being itself and Goodness itself. He suffers from none of our weaknesses, defects, or deficiencies, either physical or moral. The God who fashioned us in our mother's womb knows us through and through. As the psalmist says, "Thou hast searched me and known me. . . . Thou searchest out my path and my lying down and art acquainted with all my ways. Even before a word is on my tongue, lo, O Lord, thou knowest it altogether" (Ps 139:1, 3–4).

Because God is omniscient, he knows us better than we know ourselves. He knows not only what we are going to ask for before we ask it; more importantly, he knows what we need. God is like the spouse or old friend who has known us for so long that he anticipates what we are going to say and so can complete our sentences for us. Long prayers are not needed to make our pleas heard by God. Elaborate petitions expressed in baroque language are not required to impress God and win his favor. For God already knows our needs and is already disposed to satisfy them.

This raises a serious theological question. Since God already knows what we are going to say before we say it and what we need without being told, why do we need to pray at all? This was a question that occurred to a North African pastor named Augustine, who lived in the late fourth and early fifth centuries. Augustine wrote many books: collections of sermons, dialogues, and theological treatises. But he is best known for his spiritual autobiography, *Confessions*. Today, anyone who is anyone seems to write a memoir or autobiography. But Augustine is the one who really invented the genre. *Confessions* is, as the title suggests, a tell-all account of Augustine's childhood, his search for love to satisfy adolescent lust, and his rebellion against the simplistic religion of his domineering mother. But mostly it is the narrative of how God drew the young Augustine back to mother Church where he became a bishop and one of its greatest teachers.

What distinguishes *Confessions* from almost every other autobiography is its style. It is written as a prayer to God. From beginning to end Augustine makes his public confession. He bears his soul, in all its torment and confusion, to God and to any who would read the book. He confesses his sins. He confesses his doubts and intellectual struggles. He confesses his pride—the very pride that, in a later work, he would famously judge the greatest of the seven deadly sins.

Augustine is, if nothing else, transparent and honest about his thoughts and feelings. Because he is so honest, he even asks God what is the purpose of offering a confession to one who already knows every detail of his life. Augustine's life is an open book to God. So why write a book confessing the things that God understands more clearly than Augustine himself? At the beginning of Book 5 of *Confessions*, Augustine answers his own question:

> Accept the sacrifice of my confessions offered by "the hand of my tongue" (Prov 18:21) which you have formed and stirred up to confess your name (Ps 54:6). "Heal all my bones" (Ps 6:2) and let them say "Lord who is like you?" (Ps 35:10). He who is making confession to you is not instructing you of that which is happening within him. The closed heart does not shut out your eye, and your hand is not kept away by the hardness of humanity, but you melt that when you wish, either in mercy or in punishment, and there is "none who can hide from your heat" (Ps 19:6). (*Confessions* 5.1)

Augustine realized that prayer is not for God's sake but for ours. Our heart, our motives, our desires, our actions are, Augustine says, an enigma; we are a mystery to ourselves. But even the hardest and darkest of human hearts that would keep God out is not impenetrable. There is no hiding from God. Psalm 139 expresses the futility of hiding from our all-seeing God: "Where shall I go from your Spirit or where shall I flee from your presence? . . . If I say, 'Let only darkness cover me, and the light about me be night,' even the darkness is not dark to you, the night is bright as the day; for darkness is as light with you" (Ps 139:7, 11–12). Augustine's confession is not primarily a penitential confession of sin, but a *confession of faith*.

What makes Augustine's autobiography different from almost every other autobiography ever written is that in most autobiographies the hero of the story is the author. But in *Confessions*, the central actor is not Augustine; it is God. Augustine plays with the double meaning of "confession." It is a confession of sin—his rebellion against and resistance to God. It is also a highly personal confession of the Christian faith akin to the confession we make at our baptism. Even as we confess, as we do in the Apostles' Creed, the apostolic faith in God the Father Almighty, maker of heaven and earth, and Jesus Christ his only Son our Lord, and the Holy Spirit, so too Augustine's *Confessions* is his confession of how God acted in his life to bring him salvation. Such a confession, Augustine realized, is a form of the very worship and praise for which God made us. As he declares in the opening words of the *Confessions*, "Man, a little piece of your creation, desires to praise you. He is a human being 'bearing his mortality with him' (2 Cor 4:10), carrying with him the witness of his sin, and the witness that you 'resist the proud' (1 Pet 5:5). Nevertheless, to praise you is the desire of man. . . . You stir him to take pleasure in praising you, because you have made us for yourself, and our hearts are restless until they rest in you" (*Confessions* 1.1). Augustine's prayer of confession bears witness to the ways God resisted the proud and precocious young Augustine and by his grace showed this eager, brilliant young man that the only ease for his restless spirit, the only true peace he would ever find, would come when he humbled himself before the God who loved him.

Augustine's insight is poignant. Prayer is not about telling God something God does not know. It is not about persuading God or changing God's mind. It is certainly not about convincing God to love us and so do what we want him to do. Prayer is primarily confessing all that God has already done in our lives. Prayer as confession is therefore an act of worship, for it is a celebration of God's goodness toward us. The lover who writes a poem about the beauty and sweetness of his beloved takes delight in writing the poem and then in reading the poem to his beloved. He finds pleasure in *writing* the poem because it allows him to meditate on those qualities of his beloved that he loves most. He finds greater pleasure in *reading* the poem because he can see the pleasure it gives to his beloved. This is the essence of Christian worship, the heart of Christian prayer. This pleasure we find in confession is the very pleasure of praise for which God made us. For it is the pleasure of knowing that we are known and loved by the greatest lover imaginable, God.

A Prayer of Confession

The Lord's Prayer is not a personal confession of the specific ways God has been at work in our lives, as is Augustine's *Confessions*. But it is a confession of faith nonetheless. The faith we confess is not just our *personal* faith or trust in God. The faith we confess is the faith of the Church, the *collective* belief of all Christians. It is what Jude refers to when he exhorts Christians to "contend for *the faith* which was once for all delivered to the saints" (Jude 3). In other words, "the faith" is the gospel proclaimed by the apostles, who were eyewitnesses to the life and teachings, the passion and resurrection of Jesus the Christ. As a Catholic priest, Thomas Flynn, once reminded me, "We believe because someone else believed before us." Our belief rests upon the testimony of the apostles preserved in the New Testament. There is no way back to Jesus except through the faith of the disciples. Our faith is their faith. What we confess about Christ is what they witnessed and proclaimed.

At the heart of the apostles' faith was the new covenant that Jesus inaugurated at the Last Supper. When giving the disciples the cup of wine, he said, "Drink of it, all of you; for this is my blood of the covenant, which is poured out for many for the forgiveness of sins" (Matt 26:27–28). To put it another way, the faith of the Church that we confess in the Lord's Prayer is the covenantal relationship between God and us that was established by Christ's death and resurrection. Our petitions, therefore, are confessions of our creaturely dependence upon God. When we pray, "Give us this day our daily bread," we are confessing our need for material goods required to sustain us in body as well as soul. When we pray, "Forgive us our trespasses," we are confessing our sinfulness and our need to be reconciled to our Father. And when we pray, "Deliver us from evil," we confess our vulnerability to temptation. At the same time, we confess the God who by this covenant has adopted us as his children. For in our petitions we confess our trust in God's holiness, in God's willingness to provide our daily bread, in God's readiness to forgive our sin, and in God's power to deliver us from the evil one. The Lord's Prayer is our confession to the God who has bound himself to us in a holy covenant, as lover to beloved. We make this daily confession of faith to ground our lives in the reality of the new covenant. Confession is a form of recollection. Our prayer recalls who God is and who we are in relationship to that God. In the confession of the Lord's Prayer we remember what God has promised us in the new covenant and what God expects of us. Like Augustine, we discover that in our confession of faith God becomes present to us in our memory. The Lord's Prayer should not, therefore, be spoken in haste; it should not be something we wish to be done with, something to be checked off our list. It should, in the best of circumstances, be spoken slowly, deliberately, and meditatively, that we might savor the presence of the God whom we confess.

3

Claiming God as Father

"Our Father, who art in Heaven, hallowed be thy name . . ."

ALL PRAYER IS ABOUT God. We, however, are often tempted to make ourselves the centerpiece of our prayers. Our fears, our anxieties, our troubles, our emotions can easily take over. To be sure, our prayers, like the psalms sung by ancient Israel, are a time to bear our souls to God. In the presence of the God who knows us inside and out, we have the freedom to drop the pretense that we put on as a defense mechanism. In prayer, we can remove our public masks, the personae we adopt at work or in our role as parent at home. Because the penetrating gaze of God sees right through these, we experience the liberation of "being ourselves." Sometimes, however, we have been living in these social roles so long that we don't know the difference between our public face and our true selves. In God's presence we are given the freedom to confess our confusion about these conflicting emotions, the battle between what we are and what we think we should be. We can say with Augustine, "I am a mystery to myself." Yet, in the company of God, we find the ground of our being, the one whose grace reveals who we really are and who by his grace we may yet become. The discipline of a regular prayer life promotes the introspection and self-awareness we need to be emotionally healthy. When we respond to the call of grace to enter a time of prayer, God's grace gives us the gift of being honest with him and ourselves. Grace liberates our mind and frees our tongue to name the ugliest feelings that are the source of profound shame and are in need of healing. Graced prayer frees us from self-deception; it helps us "keep it real."

All of this is true enough, but prayer is not primarily a cheap alternative to therapy. In the hands of a counselor skilled in asking questions, we can discover emotions and their causes that we could not name on our own. Then we are able to place these emotions before God in prayer and seek his healing grace. But if we make prayer a time for self-therapy, then prayer becomes corrupted by the very narcissism it is intended to correct. For prayer is supposed to turn us from being centered upon ourselves to being centered upon God. Jesus's teachings on prayer are an invitation to an I-Thou relationship with the One who created us and called us to be his children, members of his earthly body, the Church. The call to *koinōnia* or fellowship with God in the community of faith is as intensely personal as it is corporate. There is an invitation to intimacy that draws us beyond ourselves to set our gaze upon the God whose wonder and glory can fill us with speechless awe. There is an invitation to compassionate comradeship that is attentive to the hurts and struggles of others as well as our own. But from beginning to end, prayer is about God. God is the one whose brilliant light we seek to behold. God is the Spirit who links our prayers together into a single corporate voice of fellowship and doxology. That is why the Lord's Prayer begins not with us, not with our petitions, not even with a cry for grace, but by naming the God to whom we pray. For when we confess that the God of the universe is "our Father" we name the One who is the condition upon which all the following petitions rest. Our need for daily bread, the forgiveness of trespasses, deliverance from temptation, and our hopeful expectation that these needs will be met rest upon the relationship with God implied by the words "our Father."

The Father of Israel

There is nothing uniquely Christian about speaking of God as "Father." In the Old Testament, the prophets occasionally speak of the God of Israel in precisely this manner. In 597 BC, the armies of the Babylonian king, Nebuchadnezzar, conquered the southern kingdom of Judah, razing Solomon's temple and leading the elite of Israel into captivity in Mesopotamia. There, Jews began calling themselves *bnei hagolah* or "children of the exile." Interceding for Israel, Isaiah called out to God, asking where was the God who led his people out of Egypt, through the Red Sea, as a shepherd herding his flocks. "Look down from heaven and see, from thy holy and glorious habitation. Where are thy zeal and thy might? The yearning of thy heart and thy compassion are withheld from me. For thou art our Father, though Abraham does not know us and Israel does not acknowledge us; thou, O LORD, art our Father, our Redeemer from of old is thy name" (Isa 63:15–16). Traditionally, when speaking of the father of Israel, the Old Testament authors are referring to one of two people. They may speak of Abraham, whom God led out of Mesopotamia to settle in the land of Canaan and become a great nation. More commonly, though, *father* refers to Jacob, who here is called Israel because he was the father of the twelve sons whose descendants made up the twelve tribes of Israel to which all Jews belong. Here Isaiah declares that the patriarchs are dead and can be of no help to this people in exile. God is their true father. God is the one who chose Jacob and his descendants to be his people. With them God made a holy covenant at Sinai that set them apart from all other nations. So God is their father. Although God's children rebelled and so were the recipients of his tough love, nevertheless he remains their father. Because it is the nature of a father to have compassion for his children, Isaiah calls upon God to act like the Father he is and deliver them from Babylon.

In his humanity, Jesus was a Jew. Most of his followers were Jews. Therefore, when Jesus taught, he naturally invoked the familiar ideas and images of the Jewish Scriptures. He intentionally repeated themes from the biblical narrative of Israel's relationship with God. Yet he was not merely a prophet. Jesus is the Messiah, or Christ, who came to *fulfill* the law of Moses and the interpretation of the law revealed in the preaching of the prophets. He fulfilled the law and the prophets, not simply in the sense that in him the Old Testament predictions of a messiah came true. Rather, in his life and ministry the teachings contained in the commandments of Torah and the writings of the prophets gained a fuller meaning. The Old Testament revelation was, as the book of Hebrews put it, a shadow of a higher, perfect righteousness that becomes visible in Jesus's relationship with his Father. So when Jesus invokes the language of Moses or the metaphors of the prophets, their words gain a new and deeper meaning. In instructing his disciples to address God as "our Father," Jesus echoes the language of Isaiah. He was reminding them that as children of Israel, the God who called their nation into being was their father.

Yet, because it is Jesus who calls God "our Father," he is revealing to us a whole new understanding of who our heavenly Father is. For at the same time that Jesus is fully human he is also fully God. He is, as John declares, the divine Word made flesh, the only begotten Son of God who was in the beginning with God. Therefore he is, as we confess in the Nicene Creed, "God from God, Light from Light, true God from true God." When Jesus, the Son of God, calls God "Father" he is speaking about God from a unique vantage point. He understands who God the Father is more fully than even the greatest of Old Testament prophets. As John put it, "The Law was given through Moses; grace and truth came through Jesus Christ. No one has ever seen God; the only Son, who is in the bosom of the Father, he has made him known" (John 1:17–18). In other words, when Jesus told us to pray "Our Father who art in heaven," he was not telling us to think about God as being similar to our earthly father. Rather, he was inviting us to pray to the God Jesus uniquely knows as Father. Our idea or mental picture of God the Father is not our earthly father with super metaphysical attributes (omniscience, omnipotence, etc.) tacked on. Our image or impression of God comes from Jesus himself, who is the image of his heavenly Father. When Philip asked Jesus, "Show us the Father and we shall be satisfied," Jesus answered him, "He who has seen me has seen the Father" (John 14:8–9). When we pray "our Father," we are praying to and thinking of the Father revealed in Jesus, his incarnate Son.

Jesus's Praying to His Father

The unique relationship of Jesus and his Father is most clearly seen in Jesus's own prayers. First, in Matthew's account of Jesus in the garden of Gethsemane, Jesus withdraws with Peter, James, and John, who are to keep watch while he prays. In this secluded spot, Jesus lifts up his voice, saying, "My Father, if it be possible, let this cup pass from me, nevertheless, not as I will, but as thou wilt." A second time he prays, "My Father, if this cannot pass unless I drink it, thy will be done" (Matt 26:39, 42). This Father is one who has sent Christ into the world and whose will it is that he drink the bitter cup of his passion and cross. During the fifth-century debates between bishops over the right way to think about the Incarnation, Jesus's prayer at Gethsemane was troubling. On the one hand, the Father wills that he go to his death on the cross. On the other hand, Christ the Son seems to will the exact opposite. How, the bishops asked, can the Father and Son be one God and yet have diametrically opposite wills? One solution came from an Egyptian bishop, Cyril of Alexandria. He argued that the Father and Son both will the same thing: that humanity be redeemed. Yet, because Jesus is fully human as well as fully God, he possesses our instinct for self-preservation.

Therefore, he felt the natural impulse to avoid an agonizing death. In the union of the divine Word and our human nature, however, the power of the Word, like the gift of grace, sanctified and strengthened Jesus's humanity, allowing him to resist the temptation to flee the cross. So in Jesus's prayer "not as I will, but as thou wilt," we hear Jesus's submission to the divine will that humanity's redemption come through the cross. Thus the Son's perfect obedience to the Father's will reconciles Adam's race to God.

The second prayer comes in John's account of Jesus's last night with his disciples before his crucifixion. Unlike Matthew, Mark, and Luke, John has no "last supper." Jesus washes the disciples' feet and then begins a sermon or "farewell discourse" in which he warns the disciples of the dangers and spiritual challenges they will face once he is gone. The homily ends with a pastoral prayer for the Church: "Father, the hour has come; glorify thy Son that the Son may glorify thee, since thou hast given him power over all flesh, to give eternal life to all whom thou hast given him. And this is eternal life, that they know thee the only true God, and Jesus Christ whom thou hast sent. I glorified thee on earth, having accomplished the work which thou gavest me to do; and now, Father, glorify thou me in thy own presence with the glory which I had with thee *before the world was made*" (John 17:1-5).

Here Jesus uses the language of "glory" to name his unique relationship with the Father. When he prays "glorify thy Son that the Son may glorify thee," Jesus is asking that the Father allow him to accomplish the work for which the Father sent him in order that the Father might be glorified in the fulfillment of his plan of salvation. By Christ's death and resurrection, the Father and Son glory together in their triumph over death and their deliverance of humanity from slavery to sin and death. But then Jesus prays, "Father, glorify thou me in thy own presence with the glory which I had with thee before the world was made." This glory is not the glory that the saints receive at the resurrection when, as Paul tells the Corinthians, our mortal bodies will be changed into the likeness of Jesus's glorious body, our corruptible flesh will put on incorruption, and we shall be transformed into his likeness. The glory we shall receive at the resurrection is alien to our earthly nature. We do not naturally radiate a heavenly aura. Such glory is a gift from God. It comes from without, not from within.

By contrast, the glory that Christ received at his resurrection and ascension came not from without but from within. This glory Christ first made visible on the Mount of Transfiguration when Jesus's face and clothes became dazzling white. For this is the glory proper to his eternal, divine nature—the divinity he has shared with the Father before the creation of the world, before time itself. In this petition, Jesus the Son is asking the Father to restore to him his heavenly glory that was veiled in human flesh during his earthly sojourn. The Son, who concealed his divine form by taking on the form of a servant, should now, once the victory is won, be exalted on high and glorified with the glory that of right was his. The brightness of Jesus's glory on the Mount of Transfiguration revealed his identity as the Son of God. But the purpose of this revelation was not to exalt Jesus but to reveal the Father. For the Father is God. Christ, who is the wisdom and power of God (1 Cor 1:24), is the Son of God who makes the Father known. We can rightly know who our heavenly Father is only because he is Jesus's eternal Father. Jesus's relationship with the Father is the foundation for our new relationship with God as our Father.

Naming God

The glory the disciples beheld in Christ's luminous countenance was the glory of the Father himself. It is a transcendent glory surpassing all earthly splendors. It evokes awe and wonder. In the presence of this God who is beyond comparison with anything on earth, the wise are speechless; there are no words adequate to describe God. Yet, as people dependent upon words to think and communicate, as a people who seek to call upon God in worship, we desire to know God's name. As God declares in Psalm 91, "He who dwells in the shelter of the Most High, who abides in the shadow of the Almighty, will say to the LORD, 'My refuge and my fortress; my God in whom I trust' . . . I will protect him *because he knows my name*. When he calls to me, I will answer him" (Ps 91:1–2, 14–15). Indeed, knowing God's name is essential for abiding in him.

Standing on Mt. Horeb's slopes before the burning bush, Moses asked God for his name. Moses knew the Israelites would ask who sent him to free them; he wanted to be able to tell them the name of their deliverer. God replied simply, "Tell them, 'I AM sent me.'" What a peculiar name, and what a peculiar way for God to identify himself to his people. Obviously, God did not seek the advice of an image consultant, nor did he vet the name with a focus group for their reaction. He could have said, "I am the God who called Abraham out of the Land of the Chaldeans" or "I am the one who wrestled with Jacob by the ford of the Jabbok." Or if he wanted a name that would have inspired hope in the Israelites and terror in Pharaoh, God could have called himself "The Lord, the Mighty to Save" or "The Lord Terrible in Battle." That is what Moses was looking for. Instead, God identified himself as "I AM," a name capable of kindling the imagination of philosophers but probably not that of slaves making mud bricks in the Nile Delta. Yet with this name, God began teaching us who he is. With this name, we learn what it means to live in the shelter of the Most High and to make the Lord our dwelling place. For when God announced his name, "I AM," he drew a line separating all creatures that come into being and pass away from the God who simply *is*, the one who always has been and ever shall be. Unlike us, creatures whose lives are like the grass that flourishes in the morning but by evening withers and fades, God, the Great I AM, is *eternal* Being itself. As the psalmist says, "from everlasting to everlasting thou art God." God alone is without cause and without beginning. So God alone is life itself and therefore is the cause of life for all other things that exist. When we know that God is the eternal I AM, then we realize that God is, as Paul told the Athenians, "the one in whom we live and move and have our being." "I AM that I AM" may not be the most evocative name for a deliverer but it *is* the most awesome. For when God instructs Moses to tell the Israelites that I AM is their deliverer, he is saying, "Tell them that the God who made all things and sustains all things is on their side. He who has the power of life and death is their champion. He who is Life itself is their refuge, for he will lead them from the living death of slavery into a new life of freedom."

The early Church often described the Father as the Fountainhead from which flows the divine light and life manifest in the Son and Spirit. Because the Father is the Source of life and of all goodness and virtue, Jesus in his great priestly prayer for the Church declared, "And this is eternal life, that they know you the only true God, and Jesus Christ whom you have sent" (John 17:3). When Jesus says that eternal life comes from *knowing* the Father, the saving knowledge he has in mind is not an abstract or theoretical knowledge of God—as if God were a right triangle whose geometric properties we had to figure out. The life-giving knowledge of the Father begins with our recognition that only God is eternal. All other things come into being and pass away. God alone is unchanged by the passage of time. Therefore, our only hope for eternal life is to cleave to the God who is life itself. But Christ not only reveals to us that his Father is I AM, the source of eternal life; he also gives us access to I AM. In uniting with us in baptism and making us his brothers and sisters, Christ united us with God so that we may know his name, call upon him, and abide in him. Through Christ who bears the glory of the Father, we know I AM, the one who is the Fountain of life or, in familial terms, "our Father." The Son descended to us that through him we might ascend to his Father and drink from the Fountain of living water.

Confessing the Father

The Lord's Prayer is first and foremost about God. When we begin with the words "Our Father who art in Heaven," we are confessing from the outset that the God we call Father is first and foremost Jesus's Father. Christ alone truly has the prerogative to call him Father. Theirs is a unique relationship. Only through Christ do we have access to his Father. We can confess the God who is forever veiled in his transcendent glory and mystery because he has revealed himself in his Son. Because Jesus can say "I am in the Father and the Father is in me," he is also able to declare to us, as he said to Philip, "If you have seen me, you have seen the Father." In the face of Jesus, the Word made flesh, we behold the image of the invisible Father. Our Father is the Great Commissioner. He commissioned the Son to be his agent of creation and fashion the universe. In the fullness of time, he sent Christ into the world to reveal the light of the Father, that the world might not dwell in the darkness of ignorance but in the light of the knowledge of God. This knowledge is neither esoteric nor trivial. It is the answer to the most basic questions of our identity: where did we come from and where are we going? In confessing that God is Christ's Father, we name the One who is the source of our being, the One who out of love made us for himself that we might share in his goodness and blessedness.

The Christian life is often spoken of as a journey. When early Christians in northern Italy came to the bishop of Milan, an electrifying preacher named Ambrose, and expressed an interest in being baptized, Ambrose explained the Christian life they would begin at baptism by telling the story of Abraham and Sarah. This was an appropriate beginning for these candidates for baptism. For the story of Abraham and Sarah is the story of hearing the call of God and following him to the promised land. It is, therefore, the story of a journey—a journey undertaken in faith. Their journey is our journey as well. And the best of journeys begins with a clear knowledge of the destination. The Lord's Prayer begins by naming the One who is our destination, the one in whom we shall find perfect peace.

4

Becoming Children of Jesus's Father

"Our Father, who art in Heaven, hallowed be thy name . . ."

IT IS COMMON TO hear people say, "All people are God's children." Because all people are created by God and derive their life from God, so the logic goes, then God must be like a parent who brings her children into the world, giving them life and love. This is a wonderfully inclusive sentiment that conforms to the prevailing spirit of our culture. But it is not at all what the New Testament means when it speaks of God as "Father" and of people as "children of God."

Creatures Made Children

One place where we see an explicit contrast between God's creatures and God's children is in John's Gospel. John begins his Gospel parroting the opening words of Genesis: "In the beginning God created the heavens and the earth . . ." As if to say, "My story is older than Genesis, older than creation itself, for it begins with the God who himself is the Beginning," John opens his Gospel with a flourish: "In the beginning was the Word, and the Word was with God, and the Word was God. The Word was in the beginning with God and through him all things were made and without him was not anything made that was made." The point of John's riff on Genesis is to identify Jesus, "the Word [who] became flesh and dwelt among us" (John 1:14), with the creative Word of the Father in Psalm 33, "By the word of the LORD the heavens were made" (Ps 33:6). Jesus is the incarnate Word who has existed eternally with the Father before the Incarnation, even before creation itself. For as the Father's Word (*Logos* in Greek), he is the Father's Reason or Wisdom. Paul says the same thing when he declares that Jesus is the Wisdom and Power of God (1 Cor 1:24). Therefore, Christ the Word is the governing and creative reason that orders all creation. He is the reason behind the laws of nature.

Curiously, John, having introduced Christ as the Creator, drops the theme after the prologue. The work of Christ as author of creation seems to recede into the past, and instead the Gospel focuses on the work of Christ during his sojourn among us as one of us. Why? The answer is twofold. First, he establishes Jesus's divine identity and, as Creator, his claim to authority over all creation. But second, John wants to highlight a sad irony about Christ's relationship with his creation. One of John's favorite sets of images to speak about Christ is *light* and *life*. Having said that Christ is the Word who created the world, John rephrases this description: "In him was life, and the life was the light of men. And the light appeared in the darkness, and the darkness did not overcome him" (John 1:4–5). The darkness may refer to the dark void before creation; the Word had the power to give life in the midst of nothing and so bring light to the darkness. But the darkness—and this is the tragic irony—may describe the very world the Word created. For John then declares, "The true *light* that enlightens every man was coming into the world. He was in the world, and the world was made through him, *yet the world knew him not*. He came to his own home, and his own people received him not. But to all who received him, who believed in his name, he gave power to become *children of God*; who were born, not of blood nor of the will of the flesh nor of the will of man, but of God" (John 1:9–13). The world, though created by the Word who is Light and Life, has neither light nor eternal life but remains in darkness until it recognizes and receives the Christ. For the world did not recognize Jesus as its Life, but rejected him and put him to death. John here is making an explicit contrast between the world and the children of God. The world was created by Christ but rejected him and so exists in darkness. The children of God, by contrast, are those who recognize him and confess, as did the disciple Thomas, "my Lord and my God" (John 20:28). They have received the light of the Logos and so know the Father whom the Word reveals. In knowing Jesus's Father, they have received life eternal. They become more than just God's creatures; they are reborn as his children. John's point is that being a child of God is not simply about being *made* by God, being one of God's creatures. We do not emerge from our mother's womb a child of God. We become children of God when through belief in Christ we receive a gift of power that is beyond the natural power of creatures. Praying to "our Father" is a confession that we have undergone a change—a change from being merely creatures to being children whose Creator has become our Father.

Of Water and the Spirit

What is this power? John does not tell us immediately. Instead he makes his readers wait until chapter 3, in which he recounts the visit of Nicodemus. Nicodemus was not only a member of the party of the Pharisees; he was also a member of the elite Sanhedrin Council that was responsible for regulating internal Jewish affairs in Roman Palestine. Though a Pharisee, Nicodemus was sympathetic to Jesus and believed that he was a good teacher, possibly a prophet sent by God. But because he feared censure and recrimination by those who opposed Jesus, Nicodemus came to Jesus under the cover of night. We do not know what questions were on Nicodemus's mind. Jesus does not give him a chance to ask them. Instead, he says to Nicodemus, "Truly indeed, I say to you unless one is born again, he is not able to see the Kingdom of God" (John 3:3). Nicodemus, like all of us at times, has a hard time grasping the meaning of Jesus's enigmatic, symbolic language about being "born again." Bewildered, he asks how a grown man can reenter his mother's womb to be born a second time. Nicodemus thinks that the birth Jesus has in mind is a natural birth. Yet we the readers already know from the prologue that this second birth is not a birth "from blood, nor from the will of the flesh nor from the will of man, but from God" (John 1:13). Jesus seems frustrated that a teacher of Nicodemus's standing is thinking so literally and fleshly, rather than spiritually. So he rephrases his earlier remark: "Truly indeed I tell you, unless one is born of water and the Spirit he is not able to enter the Kingdom of God. For the flesh is born from flesh and the spirit is from the Spirit. Do not wonder that I said to you that you must be born of God anew" (John 3:5-7). The Holy Spirit is the power Jesus gives us that we may become children of God. The Holy Spirit, after all, is Christ's Spirit.

In John's Gospel, there is no Pentecost story, as in Acts, when the Holy Spirit comes upon the disciples *after* Jesus's ascension. Instead, in John, the Holy Spirit comes upon the disciples at Easter. On the first day of the week the disciples are still hiding in a locked room out of fear of Jesus's enemies—just like Nicodemus. Suddenly, the risen Christ appears before them and gives them his familiar greeting: "peace." Jesus then says, "Receive the Holy Spirit," and he breathes on them. Jews thought of the Spirit as the breath of God. Therefore, when Jesus breathed on the disciples he was giving them his Spirit. As in Genesis God breathed his breath into a lump of clay to bring Adam to life, here Jesus imparts his life-giving Spirit to his followers. John locates the coming of the Spirit at Easter to make an important theological point about the Son and the Holy Spirit. The Spirit comes from Christ and is Christ's own Spirit. The very holy power that belonged to Jesus because he is the Father's eternal Son now comes to us when we receive the Spirit of the Son.

Jesus's reference to being "born of water" is an allusion to baptism. In baptism, we who in faith have received Christ (who is the Word and True Light) and made our public confession before the baptismal font now receive the gift of the Holy Spirit. And in this anointing of the Spirit, we receive the power to become children of God. Even as the disciples received the Spirit on the day of Jesus's resurrection, so too we receive the Holy Spirit when in baptism we are symbolically put to death with Christ (lowered into the water) and raised from the dead with Christ (raised from the water). When we receive the Spirit we are born anew; we are born of God. Even if we are baptized as an adult, we are reborn and become a spiritual child of God. In baptism, the Holy Spirit is united with our spirit. When our spirit is filled with the Spirit of the Son of God, we become children of God. When the Son of God, the Word who is light and life, "became flesh"—when the Word became Jesus—he took upon himself our human nature. That is, he took for himself a body of flesh and bone like ours, a mortal body capable of being scourged and pierced and killed. He took on a soul exactly like ours with the same faculties of sense perception, the same emotional capacities, and the same intellectual capabilities. He was every bit as human as we are. By becoming human, a member of Adam's family, he became our brother. When he became one of us, a great exchanged occurred: the Son of God took on our mortal human nature and gave to us a share in his immortal divinity. For when Christ gives us his Spirit, we become united with his divine Spirit. In that union of his Spirit and our spirit, we become kindred spirits, so to speak. We become his sisters and brothers. And if we are sisters and brothers of the Son of God, then we are daughters and sons of his Father. To address God as "our Father" is not merely our confession of faith in "God the Father" and in "Jesus Christ his only Son our Lord," as we say in the Apostles' Creed. It is also a confession of the Holy Spirit; for it is only by the gift of Christ's Spirit that we are able to confess that Christ is Lord and claim that his Father is our Father. For only in the light of the Holy Spirit are we able to see that Jesus is "the Son of the living God" and believe in the Father who sent him to us.

Jesus's Adopted Siblings

Being born of the Spirit does not mean that we become divine as Jesus is, however. For Jesus is Son of God by nature; we are children of God by grace. Paul explains the grace by which we become children of God using the image of adoption. In Paul's letter to the church at Rome, he narrates the work of the Christ and the work of the Spirit in the Father's plan of salvation. The Christian life, he says, is nothing other than walking in the freedom of the Spirit. Before Christ, Paul explains, humanity was dead in sin and subject to the punishment of death. In other words, our sin—our refusal to submit to God—cut us off from the One who is the only source of life. Christ comes to reconcile us to the Father and restore to us life eternal. By his obedience to the Father, Jesus the Son became the reconciling sacrifice for our sin and so has freed us from the condemnation of death. Christ has liberated us from being slaves to the law of sin and death (Rom 8:2). In baptism we symbolically have died and been raised with Christ; therefore, we "must consider ourselves dead to sin and alive to God in Christ Jesus" (Rom 6:11). If we are delivered from death by being raised to new life, then we who were dead in sin, like a drowning victim in need of mouth-to-mouth resuscitation, need to receive the life-giving breath of God. (After all, the word for Spirit in Greek is *pneuma*, meaning "breath.") In receiving the gift of the Holy Spirit in baptism, we are given new life because life itself dwells in us. To put it another way, when the Spirit of Christ, who is Life, abides with our spirit and dwells within us, then "the Spirit of him who raised Jesus from the dead . . . will give life to your mortal bodies also through his Spirit who dwells in you" (Rom 8:11). When in baptism we are united to the Spirit of Christ, the Son of God, we receive, Paul says, the spirit of adoption.

Paul's language of spiritual "adoption" goes back to the understanding in ancient Israel that the kings of Israel were the adopted sons of God. Psalm 2 was written for the coronation of one of Israel's kings. In the psalm, God addresses the newly crowned king: "You are my son; today I have begotten you. Ask of me, and I will make the nations your heritage, and the ends of the earth your possession" (Ps 2:7–8). In God's covenant with David, the Lord promised to establish David's descendants as an everlasting line of kings and make them his sons: "I will raise up your offspring after you. . . . I will establish the throne of his kingdom for ever. I will be a father to him and he shall be a son to me" (2 Sam 7:12, 14). The covenant is commemorated in Psalm 89, in which God declares of the king, "He shall cry to me, 'You are my father, my God, and the Rock of my salvation!'" (Ps 89:26). To this cry from his adopted son, God replies, "Forever I will keep my steadfast love for him, and my covenant with him will stand firm" (Ps 89:28). This psalm illustrates the character of the new father-son relationship between God and the king. God promises that his love for the king and the king's children is *irrevocable*. Even if his children rebel against his love and break the Mosaic law, God promises he will never stop loving them. As any responsible parent, he will punish them when they are disobedient, but God reassures them, saying, "I will not remove from him my steadfast love, or be false to my faithfulness" (Ps 89:33). Adoption is an expression of the binding relationship established in the covenant.

Paul borrows the Old Testament language of adoption to explain the covenantal relationship that God establishes with us in baptism. Even as the king was set apart from all others in Israel by being anointed with God's Spirit, so now in baptism all who believe in Christ are anointed with Christ's Spirit. Paul describes the liberating work of Christ this way: "When the time had fully come, God sent forth his Son, born of a woman, born under the law, to redeem those who were under the law, so that we might receive adoption as sons. And because you are sons, God has sent the Spirit of his Son into our hearts, crying, 'Abba, Father!' So through God you are no longer a slave but a son, and if a son then an heir" (Gal 4:4–7). Paul is telling the Galatians: we know we have been adopted when we cry out to God, calling him "Father." For there is nothing natural in claiming God as our father any more than there is in confessing that Jesus is the Son of God who died and then rose from the dead. Yet it is the Spirit of Christ speaking through our spirit that enables us to address his eternal Father as our heavenly Father. In prayer we claim the privilege of a child of God—a privilege that is available only to those who have received the Spirit of adoption in the new covenant.

Becoming Heirs with Christ

To be a child of God is to be God's heir. Paul says that when we have received the Spirit of adoption, becoming Jesus's brothers and sisters and children of his Father, we become "joint heirs with Christ" (Rom 8:17). The Gentiles, who were outside the covenant, have now by faith in Christ been incorporated into God's covenant with Israel. To be a child of the covenant is to be an heir of the promises of the covenant. The Old Testament speaks of God's fulfillment of the covenantal promise as Israel's *inheritance*. The psalmist declares, "[The Lord] is mindful of his covenant for ever, of the words that he commanded, for a thousand generations, the covenant he made with Abraham . . . which he confirmed to Jacob as a statute, to Israel as an everlasting covenant, saying, 'To you I will give the land of Canaan for an inheritance'" (Ps 105:8–11). The promised land is Israel's inheritance. So too, when Paul says that we Gentiles are now joint heirs with Christ, he means that we also have received the promise of an inheritance. Our promised inheritance, however, is not the land of Canaan; it is resurrection into eternal life and the blessedness of fellowship with God. Written to the churches of Asia Minor (modern-day Turkey) during a period of persecution, the epistle of 1 Peter offers reassurance and encourages them to persevere amid their sufferings. The epistle reminds them of the promise of eternal life that is their hope because of their new birth as children of God in Christ's Spirit: "Blessed be the God and Father of our Lord Jesus Christ! By his great mercy we have been born anew to a living hope through the resurrection of Jesus Christ from the dead, and to an inheritance which is imperishable, undefiled, and unfading" (1 Pet 1:3–4).

Yet, in our ordinary experience, an inheritance is a mixed blessing. The gain is preceded by loss. We do not get to enjoy our inheritance until *after* our parents have died. As children of God, our inheritance is different. We receive it not when our Father dies but when we die. Nor does the inheritance entail the loss of our heavenly Father, but the fuller fellowship with him. God, who alone is eternal, imperishable, and unfading, is himself our inheritance.

A monk in the fourth century once wrote a bishop asking about the life of Christian perfection to which Christ calls us (Matt 5:48). The bishop, Gregory, was pastor of the church in a small town in Asia Minor called Nyssa. Gregory of Nyssa, as he is known today, responded by writing an account of the life of Moses. In the account of Moses's life in Exodus—from his being raised in Pharaoh's house, to his leading the Israelite escape from captivity, to his sojourn with God atop Mt. Sinai—Gregory saw a model for the Christian's journey of faith. At the very end of this spiritual biography, Gregory concludes that Moses attained perfection because friendship with God became his highest joy:

> This is true perfection: not to avoid a wicked life because like slaves we servilely fear punishment, not to do good because we hope for rewards, as if cashing in on the virtuous life by some business-like or contractual agreement. On the contrary, disregarding all those things for which we hope and which have been reserved by promise, we regard falling from God's friendship as the only thing dreadful and we consider becoming God's friend the only thing worthy of honor and desire. (*Life of Moses*, 2.320)

Surely this is what the greatest commandment, "to love the Lord your God with all your heart, and soul and mind, and strength," means. It is to love God, not as a means to some other end, some other reward. Perfect love is our response to the Spirit's revelation of the Father's perfect love for us. Then we realize that God himself is the source of our happiness. The greatest good for which we can hope is the intimacy of friendship with our Father. This is what our heavenly Father has willed for us from the beginning.

As a parent, I have enjoyed my children at every age. I love seeing different dimensions of their personalities emerge in each stage of their lives. Yet with each stage they are one step closer to their goal: the independence of adulthood. The first time my daughter rolled her eyes at me—not deigning to dignify my suggestion with a substantive rebuttal—oh, that was not a happy day in our house. A part of me was indignant that she had been so dismissive of my sage counsel. But there was also a twinge of sadness as I saw in this gesture a foreshadowing of adolescence. I do not look forward to the day when as a teenager she is too cool to be teased or to be silly with me as she did when she was eight. Yet as painful as the teenage years may be for all of us, I also know that as she grows into adulthood there will be the possibility of a deeper friendship than can exist with a six-year-old. As children, their shared experiences with us are limited to soccer practice, Sunday school, and parents' night at their elementary school. As adults we will have a far greater set of shared experiences. These experiences will allow us to enjoy conversations about common accomplishments and struggles, books and ideas, dreams and disappointments. Yet even shared experiences are not enough for a deep and intimate friendship. For such friendship there must also be a shared set of convictions about what is good. This is the insight of the Greek maxim "Like is known by like. Like is attracted to like." The difference between a superficial friendship and the true friendship of soul mates is that the true friends are like-minded on what is most important.

In baptism God adopts us by giving us the gift of his Holy Spirit so that we may grow up to enjoy friendship with him. One of the characteristics of a child is the family resemblance he shares with his parents. Recently, some old friends whom I had not seen for years and who had never met my son asked, "How did you manage to get a son who looks like you, dresses like you, and even talks like you?" Well, he is my flesh and blood. Were he adopted, the similarity might not be so strong. Yet, because our adoption as God's children is through the union of God's Spirit with our spirit—a union in which we come to share the qualities of the Holy Spirit—gradually we come to resemble our heavenly Father and our brother Jesus. As we grow into our life in the Spirit, God's Spirit renews in us the image of God in which humanity was created in the beginning. With this new likeness of spirit, God's Spirit prepares us to enjoy our inheritance.

Praying as Adopted Children

With the words "Our Father who art in heaven" we name, we claim, we confess that relationship which God offers us through his Son, who became our brother, and through the gift of the Holy Spirit, who refashions our spirit in the image of our heavenly Father. By perfect obedience to the Father, our brother has reconciled us to God. Jesus has removed the sin that alienated us from God, the sin that cut us off from life. This is the very relationship for which God made us in the beginning. Now, through the gift of his Spirit who is united to our spirit, we become sons and daughters of the Most High.

Some names are the unique property of those who are in a particular relationship. There are some names of affection that only my wife may call me. Only my children may call me "Daddy." Such familiarity is reserved for them and them alone. While a number of men have been father figures to me, and a number of women my surrogate mothers, I would never call anyone other than my parents "Father" or "Mother." That would feel like the height of presumption. Yet that is just what we do when we say the Lord's Prayer. We are able to be so presumptuous because Christ has given us his Spirit so that we may enter into his familial relationship with his Father.

5

Children of Holiness

"...hallowed be thy name"

I GREW UP IN a family that did not generally use or condone profanity. I can count on one hand the number of times my father ever used an expletive. Well do I remember how shocked I was the one and only time I ever heard my mother say "damn." In all these cases I was the exasperating cause for their lapse. In contrast to the generally temperate speech at home, the conversation among the guys on my fourth-grade basketball team was coarse. Living at the intersection of these worlds, I developed a moral hierarchy of vocabulary. "Damn" and "hell" were on the less offensive end of the continuum and so to be used sparingly. By contrast, words associated with sex or unclean bodily functions were on the strongly offensive end and so to be avoided altogether. But then there was "taking the Lord's name in vain." That did not even fall on the spectrum; it was absolutely beyond the pale.

What's in a Name?

One of the reasons for my rigorous judgment about "taking the Lord's name in vain" was the following clause in the Lord's Prayer: "hallowed be thy name." Interpreted through the lens of my fourth-grade moral code, I took these words as Jesus's injunction against using God's name inappropriately, irreverently, or profanely. Now, given how common it is in American speech for the Almighty's name to be used often and indiscriminately as an oral exclamation point, perhaps there is something to be said for my fourth-grade interpretation. It is a reminder of the ancient Jewish view that God's proper name was so sacred that in Scripture it was represented by the unpronounceable four letters or *Tetragrammaton*, YHWH, and was never to be spoken. Instead, when speaking of God, Jews referred to "the Almighty" or "the Lord." Yet with the petition "hallowed be thy name" Jesus is teaching us something more profound than strictures on what words can and cannot be said. He is telling us who "our Father" is and what it means for us to be his children.

In the worldview of ancient Israel, knowing someone's name was power. It allowed you to invoke them and control them. It gave you access to them. For a name reveals something of a person's character, her history, her personality. When Abram and Sarai responded to God's call to leave the land of the Chaldeans and follow God to the promised land, God changed their names to Abraham and Sarah. He named their son Isaac, which means "laughter," to remind them of their disbelief. After wrestling with God by the ford of the Jabbok River, Jacob received the name Israel, which means "the one who strives with God." A teenage girl from Nazareth did not get to pick her son's name. The angel of the Lord instructed her to call him Jesus, which is the Greek form of the Hebrew name Yeshua (Joshua), meaning "Deliverer." Mary's son was named Jesus because God had chosen him to deliver the world from sin and death. To be named or renamed by God is to be marked by God for his purpose. "Hallowed be thy name" can also be translated "let your name be holy." So when Jesus tells his disciples to say "hallowed be thy name," he is not simply saying that God's name is sacred and so not to be treated casually or irreverently, though that is true. More importantly, he is telling us that when we pray we must confess that our heavenly Father is holy.

Holiness: The Language of Worship

The heart of the Jewish understanding of God is summed up in the words of the Shema: "Hear, O Israel, the Lord is God; the Lord is One" (Deut 6:4). God is one. There is no other that is God. God is God and creatures are creatures. Between them is an absolute difference. Therefore, God alone is to be worshipped. Holiness is the primary way the authors of the Old Testament spoke of the absolute divide between God and his creatures. Holiness denotes God's transcendence, his mystery, his radical otherness. In the prophet Isaiah's vision of God "sitting on a throne high and lifted up," he is flanked by the seraphim who worship him, calling to one another, "Holy, holy, holy is the Lord of hosts; the whole earth is full of his glory" (Isa 6:1, 3). Similarly, in the Apocalypse, John hears the four living creatures around the throne extolling God: "Holy, holy, holy is the Lord God Almighty, who was and is and is to come" (Rev 4:8). Holiness is the language of praise, for it sums up God's incomparable glory and eternity. When all other adjectives fail, we can simply say "Holy, holy, holy." It is our confession of God's otherness, our confession that God is beyond naming, beyond description.

The first time the word *holy* appears in Scripture is in the story of Moses's seeing the burning bush on the slopes of Mt. Horeb. When Moses ascends the mountain to investigate this strange vision of a bush that is ablaze with flames but is not consumed, he is immediately instructed by the voice of God coming from the bush: "Come no closer. Remove the sandals from your feet, for the place where you are standing is *holy* ground" (Exod 3:5). One traditional interpretation is that since the sandals were made from the skins of dead animals, they represented decay and corruption and so all that is unholy. Whatever the specific reason, the point was clear: Moses could not presume to come into God's presence as if this were any ordinary place. God is holy and the place where God reveals himself is holy. We cannot, therefore, enter God's presence casually or thoughtlessly. God is to be approached with deliberate humility, with fear and trembling, in a word, with reverence. For to be reverent is to recognize God's holy otherness. Later, when God descends to meet Moses on Mt. Sinai and to deliver the law, Sinai's summit is enveloped in an impenetrably dark cloud of smoke punctuated with occasional flashes of lightning. The Israelites are warned not to touch the slopes of the mountain lest they die. Thus is the holiness of God depicted visually in Scripture.

I suspect many of us are uncomfortable with the language of holiness. It makes God sound aloof, unapproachable, inaccessible. It makes God a thing to be feared rather than loved. When discussing the wedding liturgy with an engaged couple, I have had more than one bride and groom ask me to omit the phrase "fear of God" from the traditional charge to the couple at the beginning of the service; as one bride explained, "It's just not our style." Perhaps there is reluctance because we do not like the idea of a wrathful God, the God Jonathan Edwards graphically described in his often read, yet equally often misunderstood, sermon "Sinners in the Hands of an Angry God." We are more comfortable with the picture of meek, mild, and unthreatening Jesus holding cherubic children on his lap. Perhaps such is the picture of God we need as children or even as adults who have been estranged from the Church and God by unpleasant encounters with certain of Jesus's followers who have looked down upon us while setting themselves up as holy. The God of Sinai, at first glance, does not seem very welcoming.

Indeed, the idea of God's holiness is not for the spiritually immature. So easily can it be misunderstood and misused. But as we mature in the faith, we realize that God cannot be domesticated. God is God. The One who is Creator and Lord over the vastness of the universe is a being of unparalleled power that inspires awe and wonder. As the psalmist says, "When I look at thy heavens, the works of thy fingers, the moon and the stars which thou hast established, what is man that thou art mindful of him, and the son of man that thou dost care for him?" (Ps 8:3–4). When we discover that such a God *is* mindful of us and does care for us, then we are humbled; then we are inspired to reverent meekness. Only one who is so holy is worthy of our praise and worship, our complete and total submission. So when we confront the reality of our sin—which stands in contrast to God's purity, his perfect goodness, his holiness—we share the profound sense of our unworthiness expressed by Isaiah: "Woe is me! I am lost. For I am a man of unclean lips living among a people of unclean lips" (Isa 6:5). For us, wrath and mercy are incongruous; in God, we discover, both are expressions of his love. So we know that only a God of such awesome power and holiness could empty himself of all but love to dwell among a people of unclean lips that he might be our deliverer.

Our Covenantal Name

God is not the only one whom Scripture describes as holy. As we have seen, the places where we humans encounter God, such as Mt. Horeb, are also called holy. Mt. Zion, the hill atop of which stood the temple, is repeatedly called holy because the temple is the house of God. All things closely connected with God are called holy, including God's people. Therefore, when we confess that our Father's name is holy, we are also confessing who we are as his children. There is a difference between a child who is in foster care and a child who is adopted. In the best of circumstances, the child in foster care is welcomed into a family's home, given a place to live, food, clothing, and love until he reaches the age of maturity. But when parents adopt a child they make the child a member of the family, giving her a place to live, food, clothing, and love for the rest of her life. Although there may be an implicit understanding that she, as all children, will eventually move out, she is part of the family for life. As such, she is marked as a member of the family by receiving the family name. In baptism, we receive the Spirit of adoption and become God's adopted children. Then we too receive our adopted Father's name. We are called *saints*.

When Paul wrote letters to the early Christian communities of the Mediterranean world, he followed the traditional form of ancient letter writing that began with a salutation. In his first epistle to the Corinthians, he greets them thus: "To the church of God which is at Corinth, to those sanctified [*hagiasmenois*] in Christ Jesus, called saints [*hagiois*] together with all those who in every place call upon the name of our Lord Jesus Christ, both their Lord and ours: grace to you and peace from God our Father and the Lord Jesus Christ" (1 Cor 1:1–3). The Greek word that is translated "saints" is a form of *hagios*, which means "holy." Because the Corinthians have been sanctified or made holy in Christ, they are called saints or "holy ones."

In some ways "holy ones" may be preferable to "saints." For when we think of saints, we think of people of exemplary virtue and goodness far surpassing what we are capable of. They are people of great simplicity and gentleness, like Francis of Assisi, or heroic figures like the martyr Dietrich Bonhoeffer, or people who made extreme sacrifices to serve God, like Teresa of Calcutta. Yet, in the church at Corinth there were no Francises or Mother Teresas. The behavior of the Corinthian Christians was far from saintly. Paul had to rebuke them for being cliquish, for continuing to practice idolatry, and for having sex with prostitutes. There was even the scandal of a man who was sleeping with his stepmother. The Corinthians were perhaps the least likely assembly of believers to be dubbed "saints."

Paul's use of "saints" is not, as we may cynically suspect, a rhetorical ploy to ingratiate himself to the Corinthians, a means of softening them up in the beginning for the harsh scolding that is to follow. On the contrary, this is Paul's standard mode of addressing the churches in his mature writings; with the exception of the Thessalonians, all are called "holy ones." Paul addresses them in this way for a sound theological reason: holiness is our destiny. It is what God made us to be. As he writes in the letter to the Ephesians, God "chose us in [Christ] before the foundation of the world, that we should be holy [*hagious*] and blameless before him" (Eph 1:3–4). Even before the creation of the world, God willed that his people should be holy. It is for precisely this purpose that God created humanity in his image. The third-century bishop of Lyons, Irenaeus, explained that when Genesis says, "And God said, 'Let us make man in our image, after our likeness'" (Gen 1:26), it means that God gave us a rational mind so that we would have the capacity to know God and so grow into the likeness of his holiness. Yet with the coming of sin, we were estranged from the one who is holiness itself. So God chose to reveal his holiness and train us in it through the Mosaic covenant, which we call the law of Moses. At Sinai God delivered the law to Moses, establishing his covenant with Israel. He instructed Moses to explain to the Israelites the purpose of the covenant: "Now therefore, if you will obey my voice and keep my covenant, you shall be my own possession among all peoples; for all the earth is mine, and you shall be to me a kingdom of priests and a holy nation" (Exod 19:5–6). What would set the people of Israel apart from all other people was a holiness that would come from obeying the law. Their holiness was not for their benefit only but for the whole world. The prophet Isaiah declared that the holiness of Israel's covenantal relationship with God would make them a light unto the nations that would draw all the nations to God (Isa 49:6). The example of their holiness would be a beacon revealing God's holiness and goodness to the world.

The external observance of the law, however, was inadequate. It could not effect the forgiveness of sin, nor could it make the corrupt heart pure. But it was a shadow image of God's holiness that would prepare Israel to receive the one who is perfect holiness. In the Incarnation, Irenaeus says, Christ appeared that we might once again see in his face the holiness of God the Father. Because Jesus was son of man, as well as Son of God, we see holiness in human form. In his holiness Jesus bears the image and likeness of God that God has willed us to be from the beginning. So in Jesus's holiness we see what we shall eventually become. Therefore, when Paul calls the Corinthians "saints," he is speaking of people not as they appear now but as they shall become. In his second letter to the Corinthians Paul tells them that Christ has changed who we are by his incarnation, death, and resurrection. We are no longer strangers alienated from God by sin. But by Christ's perfect obedience unto death—in contrast with Adam's disobedience—he has forgiven the sin that separated us from God and so has reconciled us to God. The stain of sin that makes us spiritually unclean has been removed. This is what Paul means when he addressed the Corinthians as saints, "sanctified in Christ Jesus." Because we are reconciled to God, Paul says, we are no longer part of the old creation that was subject to sin and death.

Rather, in Christ we have become a "new creation." Therefore, he tells the Corinthians, "We no longer regard any person from a human point of view ... for if anyone is in Christ there is a new creation; the former things have passed away, behold the new has come" (2 Cor 5:16–17). Paul means that he no longer thinks about people as they were in the old creation under sin. This is what he means by the "former things" that have passed away. Now he sees them through the lens of the cross. He sees people as the new, holy creation we are because we are reconciled to God in the cross of Christ. Paul's brilliant insight is that the whole of salvation history from creation to the Incarnation has been about fulfilling God's desire that we would become holy as God is holy. When we confess our faith in the Holy Spirit by claiming God as "our Father whose name is holy," we are confessing that by giving us his Spirit, God has given us the power to live into the holiness expected of children of the new covenant.

Holiness in the Spirit

Paul realized that if God was to make us a holy people it was not enough for Christ to forgive our sins. Forgiveness is not the end of the story: it is just the beginning of our journey in holiness. Nor was it enough for Jesus to give us an example of the Father's holiness that we can imitate. He is indeed an exemplar of holiness. But unless holiness comes from within, our imitation of Jesus will be just that—an imitation of holiness and not holiness itself. True holiness must be inscribed upon the heart. It is an inward disposition. Our thoughts, our affections, our will must become holy—devoted to God with a single-minded purpose. If Christ is only an example of holiness that we are to imitate, then Christ is simply another law that is external. If Christ's holiness is to become an internal quality of our soul, then Christ must in some sense dwell within us. That is why Christ gives us the gift of his Holy Spirit in baptism. This is what John the Baptist meant when he told his followers, "I baptize you with water, but he who comes after me is mightier than I am. He will baptize you with fire and the Holy Spirit." What was the outward sign of the Holy Spirit at Pentecost? Tongues of fire. This is an apt image for the Holy Spirit. For when Christ's Spirit is united to our spirit then the fiery holiness of the Spirit, like a burning coal thrust into a pile of straw, ignites the whole soul, burning away the impure affections and self-serving intentions and filling us with a new, burning desire for God and his kingdom.

The Spirit is the linchpin that holds God's plan of holiness together. The holiness that God willed for us before the foundation of the world comes to us from the very Spirit who adopts us and makes us children of God. The Spirit who reveals to us that Jesus is the Christ, the Son of the Living God, and who convicts us of the reality of God's love for us is the same Spirit who gives us the power to live into the holiness of our heavenly Father. This holiness, this new life as a saint, is nothing other than what Paul calls the "life according to the Spirit." Since Christians are no longer dead in sin but are alive because Christ's Spirit is in us, Paul says, we should not live the life we did before our baptism. New life in the Spirit means that our whole life is radically reoriented: "Those who live according to the flesh set their minds on the things of the flesh, but those who live according to the Spirit set their minds on the things of the Spirit" (Rom 8:5). In other words, if Christ's Spirit is united to our mind and spirit, then we should have in us the mind of Christ. Our thoughts shift from the sinful and banal delights of the world to the higher spiritual pleasures that come from fellowship with God.

The life of holiness is a high and daunting goal. It is an ideal that stirs the soul and the imagination. To desire holiness is to desire that royal dignity proper to children of the heavenly king. It is a life of simplicity that nonetheless is more demanding than the highest forms of worldly excellence, requiring the discipline of an Olympic champion or a Nobel laureate. Precisely because holiness is such a lofty goal it is also at times a wearisome struggle. Left to ourselves, we would repeatedly fail and so give up hope. Without hope, we would give up the race.

Paul knew this. For all of his exalted description of the Christian's life after baptism, he was a realist. He described the Christian life, his own life, alternately as a marathon and a wrestling march. Yet he was confident that we can persevere because the Spirit renews our hope. This is the brilliant insight in Romans 8. Yes, the new life in the Spirit that we have received in baptism is liberation from sin and death. But it would be a mistake for us to think that baptism brings freedom from temptation and an end to our struggles. Sin is ingrained in us by sheer repetition. Unholy thoughts and desires become habits, our second nature. Sin is not merely a choice; it is our reflexive way of being in the world. Paul knew that such habits are not easily broken. The grace of the Spirit allows us to resist the habitual impulses of sin. As John Wesley put it, "Sin remains but it does not reign." We still feel the impulse of those old habits, but because of the Spirit who strengthens our spirit, those impulses need not overpower us.

Yet, even with the Spirit's empowerment, breaking habits can be a struggle—a struggle that may even make us doubt that we are different as a result of baptism. Like all preachers, Paul reassures the Christians in Rome by reminding them of how the Spirit is with them in their prayers.

> All who are led by the Spirit of God are sons [and daughters] of God. You did not receive the spirit of slavery to fall back into fear, but you have received the spirit of sonship. When we cry, "Abba, Father!" it is the Spirit himself bearing witness with our spirit that we are children of God, and if children, then heirs, heirs of God and fellow heirs with Christ, provided we suffer with him in order that we may be glorified with him. . . . We know that the whole of creation has been groaning with labor pains together until now; and not only the creation, but we ourselves, who have the first fruits of the Spirit groan inwardly as we wait for adoption as sons, the redemption of our bodies. (Rom 8:14–17, 22–23)

We need not, Paul is saying, be fearful of the struggles and doubts that accompany the life of faith. We do not struggle alone; it is not a private suffering. For all creation is experiencing suffering and is groaning under the burden of sin and the brokenness that results from sin. Yet, these sufferings and groanings are not those that marked the world before the coming of Christ. These are not the groanings of a dying beast. These groanings, Paul says, are labor pains. By Christ's death and resurrection, God has begun his new creation, which will attain perfection when Christ returns. In the meantime, we groan because we struggle against the habits of our former life, what Paul calls the "old man" that we renounced in baptism. Until Christ returns we feel weak and weary from our struggles: the struggle to resists old addictions; the struggle to love those who once hurt us deeply or who hurt us each time we go home for a visit; the struggle to be patient and not to respond to the petty jibes, criticisms, and backhanded compliments of coworkers; the struggle to forget grievous recollections of our past sins that continue to haunt our memory; or the struggle to persuade closed-minded Christians to live into the moral vision of the Gospel. At times these struggles seem overwhelming and we find ourselves at a complete loss for words. We do not even know what to pray for. All we can do is groan inwardly. These groans are our lament for the brokenness of our world because the Spirit has revealed to us the vision of Christ's kingdom. We know how things ought to be. We know how things will be but are not yet. Because we long for the holy peace that is yet to come, we cry out to our Father. Or rather, it is not we who cry out but the Spirit, who cries out for us "with sighs too deep for words." Yet, Paul reassures the Romans, these groanings will not end in the silence of death. Like a mother's laughter and tears of joy that come in the moment of seeing her newborn baby at the end of a long and grueling labor, our groans will give way to songs of praise. Then we will join our voices with the heavenly host assembled around the throne, singing, "Holy, holy, holy is the Lord Almighty."

Praying for Holiness

Therefore, when we pray to our Father "hallowed be thy name" we are confessing that who God is determines who and what he wills us to be when he adopts us. Our identity is shaped by our relationships. Because God is holy, we who have been called to be his children are called to share in his holiness. This is what Jesus meant when he declared provocatively, "Be ye perfect even as your heavenly Father is perfect." Such a confession reminds us that in order to live fully into the unique and intimate relationship we enjoy as children of our heavenly Father, we must be holy as God is holy. We are also reminded that we have already been made holy by Christ's forgiving sacrifice. The unholy, self-centered life has been replaced by a God-centered life. This is what we were made for. So the confession "hallowed be thy name" grounds our lives in the knowledge of who God is and what God has done for us. This daily confession focuses our mind upon the end or purpose of our journey—that is, fellowship with God—and the quality of our life—that is, holiness—necessary to attain that goal. But when we confess that God is holy we also confess that we cannot become holy on our own. We cannot be holy apart from the Holy Spirit. Our thinking and speaking and acting become holy when we cultivate holy habits by living in the company of the Spirit. By inviting us to share his name, by calling us to be saints, God has set a high bar for his children. But he has given us the Holy Spirit as our companion who helps us gradually replace unholy habits of thought, speech, and action with holy thoughts, holy conversation, and holy actions as we grow into the likeness of our heavenly Father, becoming the spitting image of God.

6

Praying to Our Father

PERHAPS THE MOST OVERLOOKED word in the Lord's Prayer is the one that is both first and most repeated: *our*. When the gospels depict Jesus praying, he addresses God as "my Father." But when he teaches the disciples how they should pray, he switches from "my" to "our." We address "our Father." We ask for "our daily bread." We seek forgiveness for "our sins." And we ask that God "deliver us from evil." One facile explanation is that Jesus is addressing more than one person. So of course he uses the plural "our" or "us" rather than the singular "my" or "me." This may be true in some sense. Yet earlier in his instructions to the disciples on the manner of their prayer, he addresses them in the singular. Although he is speaking to well more than one person, he says in the Greek "when you [singular] pray . . . to your [singular] Father." Jesus expects that his disciples will pray not primarily in a public setting, but privately and secretly in their own rooms with the door closed (Matt 6:6). But in the prayer he gives his disciples, Jesus switches to the plural. By teaching his disciples to pray "*our* Father who art in heaven," Jesus is making a profound point about the nature of prayer and the nature of the Christian life. Our relationship with God may be personal, but it is never *private*. Our prayer may be secret and heartfelt, but it is nonetheless *corporate*. This relationship and our prayers that are expressions of the relationship are lived out as members of the body of Christ, the community of the saints, the one, holy, catholic, and apostolic Church united in the new covenant. Yes, individually we may pray behind a closed door in the seclusion of our bedroom and there enjoy the intimacy of a child and her father. The content of the prayer may be intensely personal. But the prayer itself is never truly spoken in isolation from the rest of God's children. For God is never *my* Father; he is always *our* Father. I can never lay claim to some unique and privileged relationship with

God. His love for me and his desire that I flourish in the life he has given me are never separate from his love for and desire for the flourishing of the body of Christ as a whole.

The Temptation of Individualism

One example of a distorted, individualistic form of Christianity is expressed famously in the very popular early twentieth-century hymn by C. Austin Miles, "In the Garden":

> I come to the garden alone
> While the dew is still on the roses
> And the voice I hear falling on my ear
> The Son of God discloses.
> And He walks with me,
> And He talks with me,
> And He tells me I am His own;
> And the joy we share as we tarry there,
> None other has ever known.

The garden that Miles had in mind was the garden outside Jerusalem where Jesus was buried. The hymn was intended to describe Mary Magdalene's encounter with the risen Lord on Easter. Yet it lacks any of the details of Mary's brief conversation with Jesus recorded in John's Gospel. Nor have I ever known a congregation to sing this hymn on Easter. Rather, it is most commonly sung at funerals, perhaps because it speaks of Christ's particular love for the individual. That is an important and worthy point. To claim that any particular individual's experience of communion with Christ brings a joy that is *unique* to him, a joy "none other has ever known," is to imply that Christ privileges one of God's children over another. Moreover, it detaches the individual Christian from the body of Christ. Jesus ceases to be Immanuel, "God with *us*"; he is now "God with *me*." Such an individualistic piety is problematic, even spiritually dangerous, because it risks separating the individual believer from the Church, setting him apart from the children of God.

One of the most commonly asked questions is, do you have to go to church to be a Christian? It is a question to which a glib response is inappropriate. For we have all known people who have been deeply hurt by their experience in church. One thinks of children who have been sexually abused by church leaders whom they trusted. That is the most egregious, but there are other cases of broken trust that prove spiritually devastating. When I was in graduate school there was a church a couple of towns over that was a thriving, growing congregation. Our youth group often had joint lock-ins (overnights in the church) and joint worship services with the youth from this congregation. The pastor was a warm and greatly loved man. I was shocked, therefore, when I heard the news that one Monday morning he had a cup of coffee with his wife, walked their dog, and then went to his office, where he hanged himself. The church was sent reeling. They grieved for his wife. They grieved for him and the secret darkness they wished he had shared. But they were also angry. They felt betrayed. He had broken faith with them. For some, his suicide was so painful that they did not want to, and likely never will, return to church. Church to them is not a sanctuary but a place of violated trust and lost innocence. For some it is a place with such painful memories and unholy associations that they cannot think of setting foot in any church ever again. This is obviously an extreme example; yet it illustrates just how hurt some people can feel by churches they once loved. Far more often, people just throw up their hands and shake the dust from their feet because they are disillusioned by the conspicuous hypocrisy of church members or because of the politics and quarreling they see once they have served on a church committee. A bumper sticker expresses it well: "It isn't Jesus I have a problem with; it's his followers." This is the underlying sentiment behind the question of whether you have to go to church to be a Christian.

Unable or unwilling to go to a church, some people still want to hold on to Jesus. Christ without Christians sounds very appealing at times. An individualistic piety—"He walks with me and He talks with me and He tells me I am His own"—may stem from our negative experiences of "organized religion." It tempts us with two illusions. The first is that we are somehow superior to the rest of the folks in the pews; they are hypocrites, but we are not. The second illusion is that we can keep the hope of salvation and rest secure in the knowledge of God's love without having to deal with the messiness of living in community with imperfect saints.

Praying "our Father" should remind us that the blessings and the trials of the Christian life are neither enjoyed nor endured alone, but only within the context of the family of God. In our house, it is our practice to stand, forming a circle by holding hands, and to pray before the children go to bed. The holding hands and standing cuts down on the squirming, but it also represents our unity. We pray as a family; the holding of hands represents our connection, bond, and mutual dependence. Sometimes, however, I will have a time of prayer with my son or daughter or wife individually. It is a time of intimacy in which to speak about their particular emotions and concerns. Yet, even when it is just Thomas and me praying, we are still part of the larger Doughty and Smith family. How we pray and what we pray for are determined by being members of that family and by the love that unites us. Likewise, even as Christians praying in the privacy of our room, we are always praying as members of the family of God, members together in the new covenant.

Fellowship in the Spirit

Individualistic piety fails because it fails to take the Holy Spirit into consideration. We never have an unmediated experience of God. It is never just "me and my Jesus." There is always the Holy Spirit. We are children of God because Christ breathed his Spirit on the disciples. To live as a child of God is to be empowered to be holy by the indwelling Spirit given to us at baptism. Without the Spirit we could not claim Christ as our Lord and brother and his Father as our Father.

After all, many people of his time saw Jesus in person and heard his words with their own ears but did not receive him. They saw only his outward form. They saw nothing more than an ordinary rabbi from Galilee. They saw him, as Paul says he once did, "according to the flesh" not according to the Spirit. But those who understood who Jesus really is, who recognized him as the Christ, the Son of God, the light of the world—they saw him through the light of the Holy Spirit. Psalm 36:9 declares the promise, "In thy light shall we see light." This is an enigmatic prophecy. What is the light we all see? And what is the light by which we will see the light? Some early Christian teachers interpreted the prophet's words to mean that through the light of the Holy Spirit, who allows us to apprehend the unseen spiritual reality behind the material world we know through our five senses, we recognize there is something spiritually distinctive about Jesus. In the light of the Spirit, we see the light of the Father in the face of Jesus the Son. The Spirit reveals Jesus's full identity. Without the Spirit we remain blind and see nothing more than a Palestinian Jew, the son of Mary and Joseph of Nazareth. As Paul said, "No one can confess that Jesus is Lord, apart from the Spirit" (1 Cor 12:3). While the Spirit touches the intellect and heart of people who are not in the Church, the Holy Spirit's goal is to draw them into the community of believers who confess that Jesus is Lord and claim that God is their Father.

The Spirit at Corinth

Nowhere is the relationship of the Spirit and the Church discussed at greater length than in Paul's first letter to the church at Corinth. Paul had visited Corinth during his second and third missionary journeys. Paul had received word from "Chloe's people" that the Christians in Corinth were deeply divided. Some factions claimed a higher status because of a superior pedigree based on who baptized them. Others set themselves apart by claiming to have greater spiritual wisdom. Paul dismisses these divisions with a single question: "Has Christ been divided?" (1 Cor 1:13). The obvious answer to his rhetorical question is, "No." Regardless of who performed the baptism, all were baptized into the fellowship (*koinōnia*) of Christ (1 Cor 1:9), who alone was crucified for us and who alone is the source of salvation. When Paul says that God called us into the fellowship, or *koinōnia*, of Christ, he is imagining a fellowship or communion with Christ but also with all who are members of his body. When Jesus ascended he promised the disciples that he would be with them in the form of his Holy Spirit. Although Jesus ascended to the Father, he remains present and active in the world, working to bring in his Father's kingdom through his disciples to whom he gave the Holy Spirit. We can't be Christ's body accomplishing his work in the world unless we have the mind of Christ. The only way to be Christ's instruments and accomplish his will is to know what Christ would have us do. This is possible because we experience *koinōnia* in the Spirit (Phil 2:1). Only the Spirit, who pours the love of God into our hearts (Rom 5:5), can create a fellowship of drastically diverse individuals and bind them together by a common love of God.

To those who exalted themselves on account of their wisdom and spiritual knowledge, Paul quickly reminded them that none were wise by worldly standards. The "wisdom of men" is nothing to boast of since it is foolishness compared to the wisdom of God. So shallow is human wisdom that it is unable to grasp the higher wisdom of God. It cannot comprehend how salvation could come by the death of God upon a cross. So it calls the wisdom of God foolishness. Therefore, Paul is saying, in the eyes of the world all the Corinthian Christians are fools. Yet the "wisdom of this age" is impotent and vacuous compared with the "secret wisdom of God," which has been revealed to them by the Holy Spirit (1 Cor 2:7). For what higher wisdom is there than the wisdom that comes from God? But who can know the thoughts of God? For the mind of God, as Isaiah puts it, surpasses all that the eye has seen, the ear heard or the hearts of men imagined (1 Cor 2:9). How can one know the wisdom of God except that God's own Spirit reveals it (1 Cor 2:11)? Therefore, all the Corinthians who confess what is total foolishness according to the wise of the world have received the wisdom of God from the Holy Spirit. He who is without the Spirit cannot discern the things of the Spirit who reveals God to us. But all the Corinthian Christians have received the Spirit who interprets for them spiritual truth. Therefore, Paul blasts the source of division between the Corinthians with a double paradox. Since all the Corinthians confess Christ, which no one can do apart from the Spirit, then all of them are spiritual and have received the wisdom of the Spirit. Since, therefore, all wisdom is from the Spirit, none of them can boast as if he were wise in himself. In other words, Paul is in effect saying, "Why do you quarrel about who is wise? Such quarreling and boasting is the way of the world, the very world that thinks you are all fools. So why do you want to imitate people who think you are fools? Instead recognize that the wisdom of God—the wisdom that each of you possesses—is a *gift* of the Spirit. And who boasts of what they have received as a gift? All of you are wise and spiritual; so stop the rivalry that threatens to break apart the body of Christ."

Having said that all the Corinthians are spiritual since they are all led by the Spirit to confess that Jesus is Lord (1 Cor 12:3), Paul has to acknowledge the differences between them. The differences that matter are not differences of social standing (slave or free) or ethnicity (Jew or Greek). For all, regardless of class or race, have been baptized into one body, the body of Christ, by baptism in one Spirit (1 Cor 12:13). The important differences are the diversity of gifts within the body: prophecy, faith, teaching, speaking in tongues, interpreting tongues. All these gifts or *charisms* are from one and the same Spirit (12:4). Then Paul makes two critical points. First, "To each is given the manifestation of the Spirit for the common good [*sympheron*]" (12:7). The word translated in the RSV as "common good" comes from the verb *symphero*, meaning "bear together" or "bring together." In other words, the purpose of the gifts we have from the Spirit is not our private edification. And it is certainly not to make us feel superior to others. The Spirit confers his gifts to bring together and build up the whole body of Christ, knitting all these different people into a single community or fellowship (*koinōnia*) of believers.

How do the Spirit's gifts create one people out of many? The answer is Paul's second key point: "All these [gifts] are inspired by one and the same Spirit, who apportions to each one individually as he wills" (1 Cor 12:11). All gifts are from the same Spirit. The Spirit does not distribute the gifts equally. All these gifts are needed for the common good. All the gifts are needed to bind the children of God into a single household, a single community. But no one individual has *all* the gifts. Why? Why does God not give an individual all that is necessary for life in the Spirit? Life in the Spirit is always and only life in the body of Christ. The Spirit intentionally does not give all the necessary gifts to one person to create a mutual dependency between members of the body.

This stands in striking contrast with a prevailing opinion among certain philosophers of the first century, the Stoics. Stoicism can best be understood in contrast with another group of philosophers who were followers of Aristotle. Aristotle held that our happiness is dependent upon both our own virtues as well as external goods, such as health, wealth, liberty, and property. The Stoics asked, "Can a person be happy even when all the world turns against you?" Looking at the lives of great wise men who were persecuted—Socrates, for example—they answered, "Yes, you can be happy even in the midst of affliction because our happiness lies in our own virtue. For we can always hold on to our moral goodness even when we lose our wealth, our liberty, our health, and our property." We have the natural capacity to do everything that is necessary for true happiness, understood as being virtuous. According to the Stoics, the individual is autonomous and self-sufficient. According to Paul, the individual is neither. For the Christian is not self-governing but governed by the Spirit of Christ. (More on this in the next chapter.) Equally important, the Christian is not self-sufficient. She is dependent upon spiritual gifts that are not her own. She needs gifts that the Spirit gives to others. Out of her need for those gifts, she is bound to her brothers and sisters who have what she needs. God creates interdependence among members of Christ's body precisely so that no one will say to a brother or sister, "I don't need you" or "I am more important than you." Our spiritual interdependence causes us to cling to each other and to see our brother's or sister's salvation as essential for our own. Praying "*our* Father" is a confession of the interdependence of all Christians as children within God's family. It is a confession of our *koinōnia* in the Spirit.

Experiencing *Koinōnia* in Prayer

When we pray to "*our* Father," we realize that we are not praying simply as individuals. We are praying as members of the body of Christ together with all who are my brothers and sisters in Christ. Therefore, we are confessing that to claim God as Father is unavoidably to confess our relationship to the rest of God's children. We confess that, whether we particularly like them or not, they are our family. They are the Church. Because we are people born of the Spirit and called into the *koinōnia* of the Spirit, we have to confess dependence upon each other. My prayer is not just about me. It is about us.

When we realize the collective nature of prayer, we experience a palpable bond with our brothers and sisters through prayer. My first year in seminary was a hard year for many reasons, not the least of which was the recent loss of my father. I was tired of school and wanted to be anywhere but school and anywhere but New Haven, especially in the cold gray of winter. I had always wanted to go to Africa and had fantasized about teaching there someday. It seemed like the perfect time. So I worked out a yearlong stint as a missionary teaching at a United Methodist secondary school in Zimbabwe. I loved the teaching and was extremely grateful for the hospitality shown to me by the Zimbabweans and the other missionaries and expatriates on our mission. But there were many times when I felt alone. Home was a long way away, and at times the months seemed to pass at a glacial pace. I was truly homesick.

One of the great comforts came when I realized the significance of the "our" in the Our Father. I always ended my morning devotions with the Lord's Prayer. As I made the transition from my specific petitions to the Lord's Prayer, I learned to say, "And now I join my voice with the voices of your children around the world" (then I would name particular people and would picture their spot on the globe): "my mother in College Park, Georgia, the tutors and students of Squirrel Hollow at Unicoi, my divinity school colleagues in New Haven, Connecticut, friends at Lake Junaluska, North Carolina, and the congregation at St. Aldates, Oxford as we pray, 'Our Father who art in heaven . . .'" As I pictured those people and named those communities of Christians, many of whom would undoubtedly be saying the Lord's Prayer sometime that day, I did not feel alone or isolated. I realized that I was connected to the body of Christ. Then I discovered the *koinōnia* of the Spirit. Although I was still happy to return home at the end of my year in Zimbabwe, I nevertheless discovered that "home" in the profoundest Christian sense is wherever we experience fellowship in Spirit; there is the family of God.

7

Praying for the Kingdom

"Thy Kingdom come, thy will be done, on earth as it is in heaven."

THE WORDS "THY KINGDOM come" should always be punctuated with an exclamation mark. This is not a petition that can be said in a serene voice. It can be fittingly spoken only in a voice that is paradoxically fatigued and insistent. For these words express the weariness and urgency of the struggle of discipleship. They are the groanings of which Paul spoke in Romans 8— the groanings of disciples and indeed of all creation for Christ's return and revelation of the children of God. Paul's image of "creation groaning in travail" is taken from the delivery room. They are the groans of a mother who is both exhausted from pushing and filled with the urgent desire to see the child for whom she has prayed and worried all these past ten months. She is tired of waiting. Pregnancy was a time of joy as well as stress. Now the mother is ready to be done with being pregnant. She is ready to hold her baby in her arms where she can see that he is safe and well. She has loved what she has not seen except perhaps in the blurry black-and-white image of an ultrasound picture. Now she wants to see face to face the one she loves. So too, the disciple who prays "thy kingdom come" is praying in the midst of labor. She loves God and desires his holiness and justice. She wants to see face to face the God whom she has seen only in the revelation of Scripture through the imagination of faith. She is weary from struggling in a world that does not understand Christ's kingdom. She is weary from her own struggles against the temptations and doubts that still haunt her thoughts every day. She is ready for it to be over, ready for the kingdom to come, once and for all. "Thy kingdom come!" As followers of Jesus, the coming of the kingdom is our paramount desire, our deepest longing. The kingdom of God is the very core of Jesus's message and thus the larger context for every petition in the Lord's Prayer.

Jesus's Thesis

When John the Baptist was imprisoned by Herod, Jesus responded by launching his public ministry. John had called Israel to repent in order to be ready for the coming Messiah and his swift judgment of the nations. The first words we hear Jesus proclaim echoed John's message: "The time is fulfilled, and the kingdom [*basileia*] of God is at hand. Repent and believe the Gospel" (Matt 4:17; Mark 1:14–15). As a teacher I always exhort my students to begin their essays with a clear and concise thesis statement that sums up what they are going to say. Put it out there right up front so the reader is prepared for what is coming. Jesus, the great teacher, knows this lesson. These opening words are the thesis statement of his whole ministry. Nearly all of Jesus's parables are about the kingdom of God, or in Matthew's Gospel, the kingdom of heaven. How often does Jesus begin by saying, "To what shall I compare the kingdom of God?" or "The kingdom of God is like a sower who went out to sow" or "The kingdom of God is like a mustard seed"?

The word *kingdom*—our English rendering of the Greek word *basileia*—is misleading. For when we hear the word *kingdom* we think of a modern country like the United Kingdom or a medieval land ruled by a monarch, like the Kingdom of Cyprus. In either case, we associate *kingdom* with a *place*, a particular land or territory. Indeed, many of Jesus's original hearers had the same association. They expected him, as the long-awaited Messiah or Anointed One, to restore David's kingdom by liberating the promised land from Roman occupation. But for Jesus, the *basileia* of God refers not to a place but to an action. It is how God is at work in the world to accomplish his will. It is how God exercises his kingship over his creation. (For this reason, some have suggested translating *basileia* as the "reign of God" or "God's dominion.") Jesus confirms this meaning of *basileia* by adding the petition, "Thy will be done on earth as it is in heaven." So when we pray, "Thy kingdom come, thy will be done," we are confessing God's kingly authority over all creation. More than that, we are confessing that our Father is not the God of deism who in creation wound up the universe like a pocket watch and then left it alone to follow the natural laws and the light of reason into the future. Our God is neither neglectful nor withdrawn from his creation. Our Father is a king. As a wise and benevolent monarch carefully steers the ship of state in pursuit of justice and peace, so too God is ever working in the world, guiding it in the way of righteousness. Praying for the kingdom is our declaration of submission to God's kingship and our desire to see his work in our midst.

Seeing the Kingdom

Jesus's parables of the kingdom are a mark of his genius. They are so brief and vivid that children can hear and, at their own level, grasp his point. Yet for all their brevity and simplicity, his parables can excite the imagination and be the subject of reflection for a lifetime. That is brilliance! Any fool can say something in a thousand pages. But to convey such depth of meaning so simply and concisely is a rare gift. Yet his parables are often deceptively simple. At first glance we are sure we know what he means. But as we read and reread them we become less confident. That is as Jesus intended. At the end of the parable of the sower, his disciples are a bit confused. "Why," they ask, "do you speak to [the crowd] in parables?" Jesus responds enigmatically, "To you it has been given to know the secrets of the kingdom of heaven, but to them it has not been given . . . because 'seeing they do not see and hearing they do not understand'" (Matt 13:10–11, 13). Often the punch line of his parables is the exact opposite of what we expect. For example, there is a wedding banquet. Friends are invited but do not come. Those who are invited are unworthy to come. So the host invites the ordinary folks along the highways and byways. But when one of these ordinary folks accepts the invitation, he is bodily ejected because he does not have the proper attire for the wedding (Matt 22:1–14). This is the kingdom of God? This is how God works in the world? Very often Jesus's purpose in his parables is to shock his audience, to unsettle them. His point is that the kingdom of God is mysterious. It is not at all what they expect. Not everyone can see and share in the kingdom. God's movements and workings are not predictable. Participation in God's kingdom is only for those who have ears to hear and eyes to see.

When Nicodemus sought out Jesus, he came, presumably, with a question or two. But we will never know what his questions were, for Jesus did not give him a chance to ask them. Instead, he preempted Nicodemus with that most enigmatic of enigmatic sayings: "Unless one is born anew, he cannot see the kingdom of God" (John 3:3). Why does Jesus cut him off before he even has the opportunity to ask his question? Nicodemus's failure to comprehend Jesus's meaning proves the point. Not everyone can "see" or recognize the kingdom of God in their midst; only those who have been born anew, born of the Spirit of God, can understand Jesus's announcement of the kingdom. As Paul says, "Those who live according to the flesh set their minds on the things of the flesh, but those who walk according to the Spirit set their mind upon the things of the Spirit" (Rom 8:5). In other words, children of God who have been born anew in the Spirit see the world differently. They see it through the lens of Christ's redemptive work, through his cross and resurrection that the Spirit has revealed to them. They see in the world the unfolding of the New Creation that Christ inaugurated at his resurrection. Regardless of our lens, we can see nothing without light. For Jesus and for Paul, the Holy Spirit whom we receive in baptism is the light that gives our minds spiritual understanding. Without the Spirit, we are dependent upon the so-called wisdom of the world. It cannot comprehend the wisdom of God but views God's wisdom—the wisdom of the cross—as utter foolishness (cf. 1 Cor 1:18ff.). For the wisdom of the world knows only the logic of power and material gain.

In Plato's *Republic*, Socrates and his friends are trying to define the nature of justice. In their company is a teacher of rhetoric named Thrasymachus. Frustrated that so far he has not had center stage of this conversation, Thrasymachus interjects his own definition. "Justice," he asserts, "is the advantage of the stronger." This seems like an odd definition. What he means is that those who have power—whether it is the coercive force of arms or, as in his case, the power of persuasive words—determine what justice is, and they always set the terms of justice to their advantage. There is no objective standard of justice. Thrasymachus, as an eloquent orator, can use words as a painter uses his brush and watercolors: to create a beautiful picture of justice and persuade people that what is to Thrasymachus's advantage is also to theirs. It is to their advantage to pay him money to teach them to speak as persuasively as he in order that they may gain wealth and fame. This is the wisdom of the world that Paul has in mind when he says that the wisdom of God is foolishness to men. A worldly wisdom that knows only power and the material advantages gained by that power cannot comprehend how Christ's death on the cross is anything but an abject failure. That is not salvation, only defeat and humiliation. With Jesus's death, all hope of his kingdom dies with him. That is why the wisdom of God's kingdom is foolishness to people who lack the Spirit.

Only those who have been born of the Spirit and live in the light of the Spirit can see the wisdom and power of God perfected in the apparent weakness of the cross (cf. 2 Cor 12:9). They see how the power of God's kingdom works in earthen vessels to accomplish great things because, Paul says, "[They are] taught by the Spirit who interprets spiritual realities to those who are of the Spirit" (1 Cor 2:13). In other words, the Spirit teaches us how to see the kingdom of God, to see God working in the least likely of people because the Spirit teaches us the logic of the cross.

St. Augustine explained the logic of the cross this way. Christ conquered the devil and death first by justice and then by power. On the cross by his perfect obedience unto death he triumphed over the devil's deceit by his submission to the will of his father. This was the triumph of justice: Jesus rendered to the Father what is his due—absolute trust and obedience. Second, he conquered in divine power, the power of his resurrection. By the very life-giving power with which the divine Word created the world, Christ broke death's hold upon humanity. Christ's victory was a triumph of justice and power; but Augustine tells us it could not have been the other way around. There is a reason Jesus did not defeat the devil by a display of his power first. Since we desire power and autonomy—that is the essence of human pride—had Jesus exercised power first, we would have followed him only out of admiration for his power. We would have followed him hoping primarily to gain a share of that power. By triumphing first through the justice of obedience, however, Christ taught us to desire justice more than power. God's power, and by extension all human power, is regulated by God's justice. The logic of the cross is that victory goes not to the strong but to the just, who submit to the justice and power of God.

In grasping the logic of the cross we can see how God's kingdom, his rule on earth, is accomplished through the very weakness that the world overlooks and despises. The Spirit enables us to see Jesus's humility and obedience on the cross as a model for how God uses us in his kingdom. Then we can discern the subtle movements of the Spirit in and through the humble saints whom the world does not even notice. Jesus cut Nicodemus off at the very beginning of his visit as if to say, "Our conversation is futile. You will not be able to understand the kingdom of God that is revealed in me because you are not yet born of the Spirit." Without the light of Christ's Spirit, Nicodemus is blind to who Jesus really is and what Jesus is doing.

Nicodemus thinks Jesus is just a good teacher sent from God. He cannot see that he is much more than just a devout rabbi. Moreover, if Nicodemus cannot grasp the identity of Jesus who is flesh and blood, then he will remain oblivious to the mysterious, almost imperceptible movements of the Spirit in God's kingdom. When we pray "thy kingdom come!" we are, first and foremost, praying for the illumination of the Spirit. We are confessing that we cannot see the mysterious movements of God in the world without the Spirit who lets us understand and discern the logic of God's upside-down wisdom.

Christ's Kingship, a Present Reality

When we pray "thy kingdom come," we are confessing that in our Father's kingdom the Son, who for the sake of fulfilling the Father's will "emptied himself, taking the form of a servant . . . and was obedient unto death," has for his obedience been made king, exalted above all so that "at the name of Jesus every knee shall bow" (Phil 2:7–9). Not surprisingly, the words of this ancient hymn to Christ found in Philippians are the epistle lesson for the final Sunday of the church year, Christ the King Sunday. On that Sunday we look ahead to Christ's return when he shall establish his kingdom in the new heaven and the new earth. In the meantime, however, we recognize that Christ's kingship and his kingdom are not entirely postponed until the end of time, but are a present reality. Yet, if Christ has ascended to the Father in heaven, how is he king in the here and now? How does he exert his kingly power in the world before his second coming?

In the great Advent hymn "Come Thou Long Expected Jesus," Charles Wesley describes the present kingship of Christ that we confess:

> Born thy people to deliver,
> Born a child and yet a King,
> Born to reign in us forever,
> Now Thy gracious kingdom bring.
> By thine own eternal spirit
> Rule in all our hearts alone;
> By Thine all sufficient merit,
> Raise us to thy glorious throne.

Jesus is "born a child and yet a King" because God anointed him, as he did Saul, David, Solomon, and their successors, to be King of the Jews. Jesus is the one who will restore the line of David and fulfill God's promise to David that his throne will be secure forever. Yet his kingship is different from theirs. He exercises his kingship, Wesley says, "by [his own] eternal spirit [to] rule in all our hearts alone." In other words, Christ exercises his kingly dominion not by coercive enforcement of an external law but by the persuasive influence of the Holy Spirit—the very Spirit given us in baptism—who motivates us to obedience out of love for our sovereign Lord. Our hearts become the throne of Christ's Spirit. The Spirit frees us from sinful desires, chief of which is to have our own will. The Spirit frees our spirit to submit to the kingship of Christ. How?

All sinful passions or inclinations—including our claim to autonomy, the assertion that we are our own lord and master—are an expression of corrupt love. As Augustine put it, sin is "disordered love." It is a failure to love God and the world rightly. As Paul writes at the beginning of Romans, God has revealed his "invisible nature" and power in the visible things of creation so that all might know him and worship him. But humanity "exchanged the truth about God for a lie and worshipped and served the creature rather than the Creator" (Rom 1:25). This is disordered love. Instead of loving God above all things and with our whole being, we love things that are not worthy of our absolute love and cannot give us happiness or eternal life. Some worldly goods, like social status and fame, are illusory and not worthy of love. Others are natural goods, such as parents or a spouse or children or a vocation, and so worthy to be loved because they reflect the goodness of their Creator. But in themselves they cannot bring us eternal happiness; they are imperfect, finite creatures (or things) that will in time pass away. The parent who loves his child excessively and inappropriately makes the child the center of his life will be heartbroken when the child fails to live up to his aspirations and dreams. Even the pastor who loves her congregation and her ministry and pours her life into the church, so much so that she neglects her relationship with God, will find herself worn out, confused, and disillusioned when the church fails to bear the fruit she hoped for. Only God, the Great I AM, can give us eternal life and sustain us. Only God will not pass away. Only God who is perfectly good will not disappoint but eternally surprise us with joy. The only way sinful desires can be overcome is by replacing them with a purer, holy love. That is where the Spirit comes in.

In Romans 5, Paul makes the bold assertion that we are able to hold to the hope of the glory of God even in the midst of suffering and persecution because "the love of God has been poured into our hearts through the Holy Spirit who has been given to us" (5:5). What is "the love of God" that the Spirit gives us? The Egyptian teacher Origen observed that the phrase could be read in two ways. It can mean "God's love for us," but it can also mean "our love for God." Which is it? Origen concluded that it is both. The Spirit's light allows us to see that in Jesus's death on the cross God was reconciling the world to himself. The Spirit reveals to us the depth of God's love for his creatures and his desire that we be freed from slavery to sin and death. At the same time that the Spirit gives us confidence in God's love for us, the Spirit also pours into our hearts a new love for God. Our love for God and neighbor is a direct outgrowth of our knowledge of God's love for us. In the Spirit's disclosure of God's redemptive and life-giving love for us, we discover our absolute dependence upon God. And so we love God rightly. We love him because our life depends upon him. A love born out of a sense of profound gratitude and dependence expresses the realization that God is worthy to be loved above all things. When the Spirit pours such love into our hearts, all other loves flow from this highest and best love. When we love God above all else, we love everything about God, and thus we love who and what God loves. This is what Jesus meant when he said, "Love one another as I have loved you" (John 13:34). God's love for us is both the example and the cause for our loving others. When all our love is conditioned by God's love for us, the disordered love of sin is replaced by a rightly ordered, holy love—a love that is the fulfillment of all righteousness.

Loving God does not mean that we must choose between loving our spouse and loving God. On the contrary, loving God above all else means that we love what God loves. That includes our spouse and our children, but also our enemies and other things it is harder to love. In fact, it is only when our love for our spouse, our children, or our church is an extension of our love of God that we can love and enjoy them rightly. Only then can we love them for what they are: finite and imperfect creatures. Only when we love them *primarily* because God loves them and not because they satisfy our desires and dreams will we continue to love them even when they fail us and cease to fulfill our desire. We can love them unconditionally only if our love for them is conditioned by God's love.

Christ is King, ruling in our heart through the Holy Spirit, who not only awakens us to the knowledge of Christ's love but also arouses in our heart a proper love for God. When the Spirit fills us with God-like love, the Spirit is able to move us to act in service to the world out of the very compassion for broken humanity that was the cause for the Incarnation. The kingdom of God is a present reality when the children of God become the body of Christ animated by his Spirit to perform works of love in the world, even as did Jesus the incarnate Word.

The petition "thy Kingdom come" is nothing short of an invocation of the Holy Spirit. It is not only an expression of our desire that the Church, Christ's body in the world, be Christ's instrument in accomplishing our heavenly Father's will on earth; moreover, it is our confession that we cannot be instruments for the work of the kingdom unless Christ's Spirit rules in our hearts, not by coercive power but with the persuasive, even seductive, force of love.

8

Praying Hopefully

"Thy kingdom come . . ."

In the previous chapter we talked about the kingdom of God as Jesus's description of how God exercises dominion over his creation, how God is present *in the present*, how God accomplishes his will in the here and now. But at other times, the kingdom of which Jesus spoke is not God's rule in the present but Christ's *future* or *eschatological* kingdom. *Eschatological* is one of those technical terms that theologians and biblical scholars use that laypeople sometimes find off-putting. So I use the term advisedly. I use it because it conveys an idea essential to Jesus's proclamation of the kingdom. *Eschatological* comes from the Greek word *eschaton*, meaning "the end." Therefore, Christ's eschatological kingdom is the kingdom that Christ will establish when he returns at the *end of time*.

There is a decided shift in the message of Jesus's parables and teaching in Matthew. Early in the Gospel the parables have a this-worldly meaning. The parable of the sower (Matt 13:1–9) explains how different people can hear Jesus's same message but respond in different, even diametrically opposite, ways. By the end the Gospel, his parables of the kingdom have an eschatological focus. Their punch lines carry prophetic warnings about God's definitive rule on earth when Christ returns. Then will be the consummation of God's plan of salvation. Then at last Christ will rule; not merely by the persuasive force of his Spirit, but by divine power he will overthrow the kingdoms of the world and establish his perfect justice upon the earth. When he was interrogated by the high priest, Caiaphas, who sought to provoke him into confessing that he claimed to be the Messiah and Son of God, Jesus revealed his identity in an eschatological prophecy: "You will see the Son of man seated at the right hand of *power*, and coming on the clouds of heaven" (Matt 26:64). His return in power will bring judgment and recompense. To those who took up their cross to follow him and endured hardship and persecution for Christ's sake, he declares that the Son of man will come "in his kingdom" (Matt 16:28) "with his angels in the glory of his father and will then repay every man for what he has done" (Matt 16:27). The dead shall be raised and Christ will exert his kingly authority by separating the sheep from the goats (Matt 25:33). Each will be judged according to her use of the "talents" entrusted to her by the Master (Matt 25:14–30). The saints will be raised and will enter into their rest of eternal life in the Father's kingdom. Those who rejected Christ, persecuted his disciples, or neglected the poor will enter into perdition where, as Jesus graphically puts it, "there will be weeping, and wailing, and gnashing of teeth." Jesus tells his disciples that the kingdom will come suddenly, when they least expect it. We should not, therefore, become complacent because Christ's return is delayed and think we have the liberty to act unjustly (Matt 24:45–51). Rather, we must be vigilant, like maidens who are to attend to the bridegroom at his marriage feast, waiting and watching, ready to receive Christ our Bridegroom (Matt 25:1–13). Praying "Thy kingdom come!" expresses an eagerness and watchfulness like that of the attentive maidens in the parable.

Missing the Point

We Christians frequently make one of two mistakes when thinking about Christ's return and his eschatological kingdom. The first is that we often develop an excessive curiosity about *when* the kingdom will come and *what* our life will be like when it does. Will the rapture take place before or after the second coming? Will there be a second chance for people who were not taken? What will our resurrected bodies be like? Very often the questions arise not from our reading of Jesus's teaching in the gospels but from the Revelation to John. The problem with this line of reasoning is that the kingdom of God becomes such a future, otherworldly reality that it becomes wholly divorced from our life in the present. When we become so future focused we neglect our duties in the here and now.

In the 1980s, Ronald Reagan's Secretary of the Interior was James Watt. Mr. Watt was an evangelical who believed that Christ's return was imminent. His critics charged that his indifference to promoting conservation of natural resources was the result of belief in Christ's imminent return—as if that frees us from our Christian duty to be good stewards of God's creation.

We are by no means the first to make this mistake. In Luke's account of Jesus's final moments with the disciples before his ascension to the Father, the disciples asked, "Will you at this time restore the kingdom to Israel?" In other words, they wanted to know if Christ would now fulfill their messianic expectations and establish the kingdom of God that he had been preaching for the whole of his ministry. Jesus's reply is telling: "It is not for you to know the times and seasons which the Father has fixed . . . But you shall receive power when the Holy Spirit has come upon you; and you shall be my witnesses in Jerusalem, and in all Judea and Samaria and to the ends of the earth" (Acts 1:7–8). In other words, the disciples are not to worry about *when* the eschatological kingdom will come. Jesus even goes so far as to say that he himself does not know; only the Father knows. Rather, the kingdom of God that they will see is the power of the Holy Spirit, who will equip them for the work of bearing witness to the new reality that began with Christ's triumph over death on Easter.

What is the chief characteristic of the Spirit who descended on the apostles and whom we receive at baptism? Mystery. As Jesus described the Spirit's movements to Nicodemus, "The wind blows where it will, you hear the sound of it, but you do not know whence it comes and whither it goes— so it is with everyone born of the Spirit." To be a child of God, born of the Spirit, is to live as a subject in the Spirit's kingdom. Like any servant of a king, our life is not our own. We go and do as the king commands. So too, in the kingdom of the Spirit, we are blown where the Spirit wills and carried on the breeze of his holy inspiration; and where the Spirit will blow us, we neither know nor can anticipate.

In the 1990s, Greg Jenks was a United Methodist pastor comfortably serving a suburban congregation outside of Raleigh, North Carolina. A girl in his congregation had become concerned about the victims of the AIDS pandemic in Africa, specifically those children who were orphaned when their parents died of AIDS. She wanted to go to Africa and see for herself and give what help she could. The challenge was persuading her loving and protective parents to let her go. This she asked Greg to do. Marshaling careful arguments for the importance of this mission and of following the call of the Holy Spirit, he succeeded, and she headed off to Zimbabwe, where there were some eight hundred thousand AIDS orphans. When she returned and told Greg about the plight of the orphans, she asked him why he did not go too. Greg had no good answer. He discerned the Spirit calling him to leave the secure and comfortable, though demanding, life of a suburban pastor to begin a ministry for AIDS orphans. With the support of his bishop and the United Methodist churches of the North Carolina Conference, Greg founded ZOE Ministries, which began raising funds for AIDS orphans in Zimbabwe. Now he has expanded its ministry into Rwanda, Kenya, Tanzania, and Uganda, establishing orphan communities where teenagers and children work together to create self-sufficient enclaves that provide food, housing, and education for these often forgotten victims of AIDS. Greg never foresaw where the Spirit would lead him. He never imagined that he would give up one ministry to become an entrepreneur for the kingdom. Such is the mysterious way of the Spirit.

It is a dangerous thing to pray "thy kingdom come," for with those words we surrender ourselves to this unpredictable Spirit. We open ourselves to being blown wherever the world needs someone to bear witness to the gospel. We confess that our lives belong to Christ, who redeemed us with his blood and has given us new life in his Spirit. But we also confess Christ's kingly authority to do with us as he wills. As Christ's Spirit sent the disciples to the ends of the earth to be his witnesses and all but one were martyred, so too we confess that he may lead where we do not always want to go and call us to sacrifice our money, possessions, security, prestige, time, relationships, even our lives. In praying "thy kingdom come" we accept Christ's absolute and unconditional claim upon our lives. Yet we do so in confidence as we remember Jesus's promise that "those who save their lives will lose them. But those who lose their lives for my sake will find them" (Luke 9:24). For we find our life is hidden in Christ "[in whose Kingdom] moth nor rust consumes and where thieves do not break in and steal" (Matt 6:20).

Spiritually Nearsighted

If the first mistake we make in our thinking about Christ's eschatological kingdom is an excessive curiosity, the second mistake is the exact opposite: complete indifference to the future kingdom in favor of a wholly this-worldly kingdom. Such a view places apocalyptic prophecies in the same category as accounts of Jesus's walking on water or raising the dead and other miracles. They are viewed as reflecting an ancient and outmoded worldview to which modern readers cannot subscribe. Jesus, according to this perspective, is not the Son of God but a prophet or great moral teacher. The kingdom of God is realized on earth when we, his modern disciples, obey his instructions to love our enemies, to feed and clothe the poor.

When we ignore the eschatological dimensions of Jesus's kingdom, we subscribe to a deistic view of a God who, having created the world and set it in motion, withdraws his hand, becoming largely uninvolved—except perhaps by exerting moral influence through great teachers—in the lives of his creatures. Such a God may guide his people but ultimately does not "break into" history, instead leaving humanity to its own devices, living with the outcome of its free choices. Such a view is not new. It grew out of Enlightenment confidence in human progress. Having been under the tutelage of faith, intellectuals of the seventeenth and eighteenth centuries claimed, humanity now with the discovery of reason has grown from childhood to adulthood and so is able to govern itself by the light of reason without the aid of religion. Perhaps religion might be retained if it were purified of ancient superstition. There was tremendous confidence, particularly among Protestants, that European culture, emerging from the "Dark Ages" under the rule of kings and popes, was entering an age of enlightened liberal democracy. Humanity, as a race, was literally on the cusp of achieving perfection. God did not need to intervene in history. Rather, we had the ability to establish the kingdom of God on earth by electing the right leader, voting for the right initiative, and instituting social reforms.

Then came World War I, "the war to end war" that left sixteen million soldiers dead on the battlefields of Europe and Africa and ten more million civilians dead from starvation and the destruction of cities and farms. World War I was followed by the Great Depression and the rise of fascism in Germany and Italy and of communism in Russia. To the death toll of the Second World War (a mind-boggling sixty-two to seventy-eight million people worldwide) should be added the fifty million who were killed or who died from starvation between 1949 and 1975 in Mao Zedong's People's Republic of China, the 1 to 1.5 million killed in the Armenian genocide in the early twentieth century, the eight hundred thousand slaughtered in three months during the Rwandan genocide, the ethnic cleansings in the Balkans and Darfur Sudan, plus the annual 1.2 million lives cut short *in utero* in the United States. Taken together, the death toll due to war and state-sponsored violence in the twentieth century—a century celebrated as one of great progress and innovation—makes it easily the bloodiest century in human history. And this does not even begin to touch upon the environmental damage our greed and culture of consumption have inflicted upon the earth. Far from establishing the kingdom of God, we have turned God's good creation into a realm of perdition. Without the biblical vision of God's definitive interruption of human history at Christ's return and the establishment of his eschatological kingdom, human history is not the story of unending progress but merely an endless cycle of petty dictators who would rather see their people butchered and their land reduced to ashes than give up their precious power.

The prayer "thy kingdom come" is as much a cry of desperation as it is a confession of faith. This petition is a heartfelt admission that we cannot establish the kingdom on our own. We confess our weariness and weakness and insufficiency. It lies beyond our power to fashion for ourselves Revelation's vision of the new heaven and new earth. Justice will flow down like streams of water and the people will live in peace only when God breaks into history to end our warring madness. It would be wrong to think that our petition motivates God to act, to get off his divine duff and do something. There is an ancient Chinese proverb that says, "When the student is ready, a teacher will appear." So too, only when we abandon the hubris of the Enlightenment and recognize our own inadequacy and absolute dependence on God are we ready to receive God as our king and live under his benevolent dominion. "Thy Kingdom come!" is our confession that we are ready to let God be Lord.

From Optimism to Hope

The Enlightenment was an age of boundless optimism that gave way to a cynicism born of disillusionment in the face of failure. The gospel offers an alternative to either worldly optimism or cynicism: hope. Hope is at the very heart of the Christian vocation, that life to which God has called his people. At the beginning of Ephesians, Paul tells his readers,

> I do not cease to give thanks for you, remembering you in my prayers, that the God of our Lord Jesus Christ, the Father of glory, may give you a spirit of wisdom and of revelation in the knowledge of him, having the eyes of your hearts enlightened, that you may know what is the hope to which he has called you, what are the riches of his glorious inheritance in the saints, and what is the

immeasurable greatness of his power in us who believe, according to the working of his great might which he accomplished in Christ when he raised him from the dead and made him sit at his right hand in the heavenly places, far above all rule and authority and power and dominion, and above every name that is named, not only in this age but also in that which is to come. (1:16–21)

Paul's unceasing prayer is that God will illuminate the minds of those whom he calls to be saints. He prays that God will reveal to them "the hope of their calling." In the New Testament, hope can be an *action* or an *object*. As an action, "hoping" is quite different in the New Testament than in our colloquial usage. "Hope" for us is a synonym for "wish," as when we say, "Oh, I hope it doesn't rain during Saturday's game!" This is a mere wish. There is absolutely no relationship between my desire that the game not be rained out and whether or not it actually will be. In the New Testament, by contrast, hope is the *confident expectation* of the future fulfillment of God's promise. Such hope is more than wishful thinking because it is grounded in the reasonable belief that in due season God, who has been faithful to his people in the past, will accomplish what he has promised.

Hope as an object refers to *that for which we hope*. It is the content of God's promise. Here in Ephesians Paul is saying that God's children, who are called to bear the name "saint" and to live into his holiness, also have the hope of a "glorious inheritance," namely, the hope of resurrection to eternal life. Since we know that God's power is at work in us—the very power that raised Jesus from the dead—we can be confident that God will also raise us from the dead. And as Christ at his resurrection put on his heavenly glory, so too we shall be clothed with his glory at our resurrection. What is the glory that is our inheritance as saints and children of God? It is the glory of the Father. When we are raised from death to life in God's eschatological kingdom, God himself becomes our eternal dwelling place. That is strikingly different than our lives at present. Now our minds are scattered and our attention divided. Even when we have a deep love for God, we are often so busy focusing on the many mundane details of life, some important but many more trivial, that our minds are not able to focus on God all the time. But in Christ's kingdom, Paul says, God shall be "all and all." Gregory of Nyssa interpreted this to mean that God will be everything to us: our home, our nourishment, our drink, and our light. Then God is present to our thoughts at all times and in all places. God completely fills our mind. This is what it means to abide in God, to dwell in his presence. Our mind is like a mirror that reflects an image of what we love and of that which is at the center of our thoughts. Our life—what we talk about, what we do in our free time—is an outward reflection of our mind. For example, one whose mind is set on money constantly worries about and talks about money and is often fearful of losing it. Even his face bears the lines of worry that reveal his preoccupation with money. So too, when in the kingdom God shall be "all and all" and shall be the ever-present object of our thoughts, then our face—like the face of Moses, who stood in the presence of God on Mt. Sinai—will be transformed, mirroring the glory of our Father.

But that is then. This is now. We do not now enjoy the blessedness of beholding the splendor of God's glory. It is our hope and not a present reality. Yet, as a people who have experienced the life-changing power of God, we wait in the confidence of hope. And that confidence makes all the difference in how we live in the present. It means we *live hopefully*. That is, we live in the here and now with our eyes firmly fixed on the prize. And so, like an Olympic athlete who lives each day in preparation for the games and her chance to win a medal, our lives are oriented to our goal, our inheritance.

Writing from prison in Rome, Paul bared his soul to the Christians at Philippi. This letter provides profound insight into the nature of the Christian life, into the tension Christians feel between our love of our present life of service to God and our hope for the greater blessedness in the kingdom to come.

> Not that I have already obtained this or am already perfect; but I press on to make it my own, because Christ Jesus has made me his own. Brethren, I do not consider that I have made it my own; but one thing I do, *forgetting what lies behind and straining forward to what lies ahead*, I press on toward the goal for the prize of the upward call of God in Christ Jesus. Let those of us who are mature be thus minded; and if in anything you are otherwise minded, God will reveal that also to you. Only let us hold true to what we have attained.
>
> Brethren, join in imitating me, and mark those who so live as you have an example in us. For many, of whom I have often told you and now tell you even with tears, live as enemies of the cross of Christ. Their end is destruction, their god is the belly, and they glory in their shame, with minds set on earthly things. But *our commonwealth [politeia]* is in heaven, and from it we await a Savior, the Lord Jesus Christ, who will change our lowly body to be like his glorious body, by the power which enables him even to subject all things to himself. (Phil 3:12–21)

The perfection of the resurrection, of Christ's eschatological kingdom, is not now. Yet Paul strives for it by leaving behind the old life that was oriented entirely to this world and made an idol of food and other earthly things. He does so because he knows that "our commonwealth" is not here but in heaven. The Greek word *politeia*, from which we get our words *polity* and *politics*, was a technical term for "citizenship." In the ancient Greek world, one's city meant more than simply the place where one lived. It had its own history and culture that defined the identity of its citizens. One's *politeia* was the place of one's identity. Therefore, when Paul says, "our *politeia* is in heaven," he means that our identity lies not in this world but in the kingdom of God. When our identity, our sense of self, is "in heaven," it changes the way we view our life on earth and so the character of that life. We live as "aliens and exiles" (1 Pet 2:11), as sojourners in a foreign land.

The Christian whose *politeia* is in the kingdom of heaven has a similar experience. Having received a vision of Christ's kingdom contained in the poetic prophecy of Isaiah or the parables of Jesus, we are grieved when we see how far the world is from what it shall be. We feel like strangers in a foreign land when we realize how different our understanding of what is real is from the secular, scientific worldview that is normative for public discourse in the media. The world mistakes glamour for glory and is blind to the beauty of humility. It defines success in terms of wealth and so does not recognize the richness of the simple life. Our priorities are different. I teach at a university that has one of the best basketball programs in the country. I've been a fan for almost thirty years. Yet it troubles me to see the host of students who are willing to camp out in all sorts of weather for six weeks to get tickets to the Duke-Carolina game, while so few students attend worship services at Duke Chapel. We often do not feel at home in any political party. For no one political platform is an adequate expression of a Christian moral vision. Our understanding of justice and liberty is foundationally different. And so too is the locus of our hope. I have good friends for whom politics is virtually a religion. When their party wins, they are ecstatic and filled with confidence for the future. But when their party loses, a pall descends on their house for days after and there is literally the shedding of tears. Yet Christians, whose citizenship is in heaven, remember the words of the psalmist: "Put not your trust in princes, in a son of man, in whom there is no help. [For] when his breath departs he returns to his earth; on that very day his plans perish" (Ps 146:3–4). Such is the transitory nature of even the well-intentioned political programs. As "resident aliens," we are not *uninvolved* in the politics of this world. We must work to promote justice, as the prophets of ancient Israel exhort us. But we work for justice confident that it is the Holy Spirit working in and through us who will bring signs of the kingdom in our world. Yet while we work for justice, we are deeply conscious that whatever justice we can accomplish is but a pale imitation of the true and perfect justice that awaits us in Christ's eschatological kingdom.

Because we live as "aliens and exiles" we pray "Thy kingdom come!" with an urgency of tone characterized by joy tinged with melancholy. Because we must wait in a world that does not understand us, that does not share our values or our hope, the melancholy that accompanies our petition expresses a spiritual homesickness. It conveys a longing for our true fatherland, for our *politeia*. Yet there is also joy. For we, like children on Christmas Eve, are filled with excitement for the glorious inheritance that will come soon. Such joy is truly hopeful joy because we are confident that the God who triumphed over the powers and principalities of this world, even over death itself, will in time complete the transformative work he began on Good Friday and Easter. In short, praying for Christ's heavenly kingdom on earth expresses the deep paradox of Christian hope: while we celebrate and live boldly into the kingdom that Christ has already inaugurated through the giving of his Spirit, we must still wait. And while we wait, our prayer is for its eschatological consummation.

9

Hungry for Bread

"Give us this day our daily bread."

OFTEN WHEN WE START to pray, we get all *spiritual*. Since prayer is a time of stepping back from the mundane, of turning from the distractions of the world to center our minds in God, it is natural that we think our speech and our meditations should be "better" than the ordinary. Paul, as we saw earlier, observed that those who walk according to the flesh set their minds on the flesh and those who walk according to the Spirit set their minds upon spiritual things. Since prayer is the time when our spirit communes with Christ's Spirit, it makes sense that in prayer our mind becomes set on the things of the Spirit. Our words should be holy and our thoughts lofty. We become, in a word, "spiritual." At times we, especially those of us in the clergy, become grandiloquent and sagely. Other times we may get all meek and lowly. Even the tone with which we pray may become hushed and airy. This, after all, is what we think God expects of us. Yet there is a real danger here. Often our prayers can become so "spiritual" that they are wholly disconnected from the rest of our life. We sound more like angelic beings whose feet do not tread upon the earth than simple creatures trying to live faithfully into our holy calling amid the tedious demands of day-to-day routine and hidden temptations. Ironically, one of these is the temptation to be spiritual.

The Temptation to Be Spiritual

C. S. Lewis's classic *The Screwtape Letters* purports to be a collection of newly discovered letters from a senior devil, Screwtape, advising his nephew, Wormwood, how to ensnare the soul of a mortal. Presenting the Christian journey from the perspective of a demonic tempter, Lewis offers penetrating insights into the nature of temptation. In one especially profound letter, Screwtape, having received the lamentable news that Wormwood's "patient" has begun praying, counsels his nephew to make his man's prayers spiritual. They should be full of lofty sentiments and the people for whom he prays so idealized that he is praying for phantoms instead of the people themselves. Screwtape illustrates his point by recounting one patient some years before whose mother was particularly intrusive and aggravating and, at times, hard to love. The Enemy (i.e., God) put it into the patient's head to try praying for his mother, and it looked like the Enemy had won. But Screwtape prevailed in the end by getting the silly man to pray for such a spiritualized version of his mother that he was not really praying for his mother at all. His prayer was so disconnected from reality that if his real mother accidentally interrupted him in the middle of prayer—even in the very moment in which he was praying so sweetly and piously for her—he would snap her head off for having disturbed him. Instead of learning to be patient with the flesh-and-blood woman who cooked his meals and washed his clothes but irritated him by her constant complaining about her arthritis or his friends whom she did not like, he grew to loathe her even more than he had before. He loathed her precisely because the idealized, spiritualized version of his mother who was the object of his prayer only highlighted the annoying quirks and moral failings of his real mother. So spiritual was his prayer that it was utterly counterproductive.

If, however, prayer is about what is most real; if prayer is a confession of faith that allows us to live into the reality of the new covenant we confess; if prayer is a surrendering to the Spirit's dominion so that the kingdom may be realized on earth; if prayer is seeking the grace to live into holy relationships with real people, as well as with God, then our prayer must be, as Christian mystics have described it, like Jacob's ladder with its feet firmly anchored on earth and its arms grasping for heaven. Prayer must be in touch with our lives in the here and now at the same time that it speaks of our eschatological hope for the new heaven and the new earth. For truly spiritual prayer—prayer in which Christ's Spirit makes our will conform to his will—is not a means of *escaping* the world but the means of *sanctifying* our lives *in the world*. So it must be fully connected to both the mundane and the transcendent. The people for whom we pray cannot be figments of our high-minded fantasy: spiritual pinup girls, people as we wish they were. They must be people like us: flesh-and-blood human beings with bad breath, poor grammar, annoying habits, and mixed motives. Likewise, we must pray for ourselves as we really are. In order to open ourselves to the healing and transformative grace of the Holy Spirit, we, like any patient, have to tell the great physician "where it hurts." We must confess who we are on this side of the glory of the resurrection. We have to name our creaturely needs and how the goodness of what God made us to be has been corrupted by sin. This is precisely what Jesus does in his prayer.

"Give us this day our daily bread." What is this bread that is the object of our prayer? Now, the word *bread* in the New Testament has a polyvalence of meaning. It can refer simply to bread, such as the little boy's barley loaves with which Jesus fed the five thousand or the unleavened bread that Jesus blessed and broke at the Last Supper. At other times *bread* is used metaphorically to refer to Jesus himself ("I am the bread of life" [John 6:35]) or Jesus's flesh ("I am the living bread come down from heaven . . . the bread which I shall give for the life of the world is my flesh" [John 6:51]). Indeed, the word of God is likened to bread that gives life for the soul, as when Jesus, countering the devil's suggestion that he end his fast by turning stones into bread, retorts by quoting Deut 8:3: "Man does not live by bread alone but every word that proceeds from the mouth of God" (Matt 4:4). Therefore, it is reasonable to interpret the "daily bread" for which we are to pray as including the word of God or the bread of heaven that is Christ's flesh. But if we jump too quickly to this spiritual meaning of bread, bypassing the literal or material meaning of "bread" as bread or more generally food for the body, then we miss completely the relationship between the everyday and the eternal, the earthly and the heavenly, that Jesus is teaching us through the Lord's Prayer.

Up to this point in the Lord's Prayer, the focus has been heavenly and the tone spiritual. We have confessed our relationship with our Father. We have claimed the goal of imitating his holiness. We have cried out for his kingdom to come upon the earth. With this last petition, "on earth as it is in heaven," Jesus explicitly links the mundane and the heavenly, the transitory and the eternal. He wants us to realize that the life of discipleship is lived at the intersection of earth and heaven. The holiness of our heavenly Father becomes the character of Christ's earthly kingdom. Being spiritual, therefore, can never be abstracted or disconnected from our everyday life. For being truly spiritual is about being led by the Spirit, who sanctifies every movement of our life with his presence. There is no distinction between the trivial and the monumental. The simple experience of eating a meal or laughing with friends over a good story can be spiritual if we discern the Spirit's presence. Conversely, a moment of paramount significance, such as a wedding, can be spiritually empty if we are so distracted by the frills of the occasion that we do not seek the Spirit. So now the focus of the Lord's Prayer shifts. Its petition is as down-to-earth as you can get: "Give us this day our daily bread." What could be more basic than bread? What could be more mundane and ordinary?

Fruit of the Earth

Later in the Sermon on the Mount, Jesus counsels his followers about the importance of living in the present and not being preoccupied with the future. He warns against being overly concerned for the things of the body: "Is not life more than food, and the body more than clothing? Look at the birds of the air: they neither sow nor reap nor gather into barns, and yet your Father feeds them. Are you not of more value than they? . . . Therefore, do not be anxious, saying, 'What shall we eat?' or 'What shall we drink?' . . . For the Gentiles seek all these things and your heavenly Father knows you need them all. But seek first his kingdom and his righteousness, and all these things shall be yours as well" (Matt 6:25–26, 31–33). The life to which Jesus calls us is not preoccupied with the things that occupy the world's attention. Our Father knows we need food and will provide for our bodily needs, as would any good parent. Why then does Jesus, a few verses earlier, tell us to ask for our daily bread? Once again, the petition is not necessary to remind God of our needs. Rather, it is our confession of our dependence upon the earth for life-giving food. Why is such a confession necessary? Why do we need to be commanded to pray for food? After all, for a country of people arguably overfocused on food, such instruction seems superfluous. The reason for this confession is not that we fail to think about food but that we fail to think about food *rightly*.

Food, or more precisely thinking and desiring food righteously, is a spiritual challenge that every generation has faced. Paul describes those who have an excessive and unhealthy desire for food as being guilty of a form of idolatry: "Their god is the belly, their glory in their shame, with minds set on earthly things" (Phil 3:19). When Jesus illustrates the hubris of human aspirations to self-sufficiency, he tells a parable of a man who built barns to store all his grain so that he might take his ease, secure in his wealth (Luke 12:13–21). So too we citizens of the West in the twenty-first century have our own issues with food. Norman Wirzba, in an essay titled "The Grace of Good Food," describes how distorted our thinking about food has become. This disorder is traceable, in part at least, to a cultural and demographic shift in America over the last two hundred years. In 1790, 90 percent of American workers made their living by farming. Even professionals like lawyers, teachers, and clergymen, who lived in town, owned farms. In 1900, 40 percent of Americans worked on farms. On the eve of the twenty-first century, out of a total workforce of 129 million, only 775,218, or .5 percent, of responders to the 2000 census listed their occupation as farmer or farm manager. This change was made possible in large part by technological advancements (the McCormick reaper in 1831, John Deere's steel plow blades in 1837, the shift from horses to automotive tractors and combines between 1917 and 1930) that produced an agricultural revolution. In 1800, one farm was needed to produce enough food for two families. A hundred years later one farm could feed six families. By 1930, one farm could produce enough to feed eleven families. This increase in productivity gave more people the option of leaving the farm, moving to the city, and finding positions in industry or service-sector jobs, which in turn has caused the United States to shift from being a largely rural to a predominantly urban society.

One result of this demographic shift is that the vast majority of the U.S. population has become disconnected from the source of its food. We do not see the fields where the crops are grown, the pens or stalls in industrial-sized barns where the majority of cows, pigs, and chickens are raised. Out of sight, out of mind. It is a common phenomenon that when elementary school children are asked the simple question, "Where do we get our food?" their first answer is "from a grocery store." Of course, they eventually say "farm." But their initial answer is revealing. As Wirzba observes, we think of food chiefly as a *commodity* to be bought and sold rather than grown and harvested. Consequently, we do not see how our lives are tied to God's creation. Most of us urbanites and suburbanites check the morning weather report to determine whether we should take an umbrella to work or whether we will need to wear a coat. But for a farmer, the weather has everything to do with when she should plant her crops, whether the crops will survive, and whether she will make enough from her harvest to pay the mortgage on the farm. Farmers have a deep sense of how dependent they are upon the forces of nature for their survival. Those of us who do not live in rural communities tend to be disconnected from the earth and from the people who grow and harvest the food we need for survival. When we think of food as a mere commodity that we gain by merely opening our wallets, we begin to think of ourselves as standing *above creation*. This is even more the case when the food we eat is processed and prepackaged. Then food is thought of as a manufactured good the nutritional content of which we are free to manipulate to satisfy current consumer sensibilities about health and taste.

Child of suburbia that I am, I have never gone hunting. Although my grandfather hunted wild boar in the mountains of eastern Kentucky and Tennessee, hunting was a tradition that was not carried on by the next generation of Smiths. Partly that was due to where we lived; there was no place near my Atlanta home to go hunting. In fact, I must admit, as a boy I took a rather superior attitude toward people who hunted. What sort of person, I thought, takes pleasure in killing animals? When I was in graduate school I worked at a summer camp. Wonderful friendships can emerge out of the "camp experience," and one of the friendships I struck up was with Ralph. Although Ralph lived in suburbia, he was a country boy at heart and one of his passions was hunting. He hunted with both shotgun and a bow. When I listened to Ralph talk about hunting, he spoke eloquently and with reverence about the buck he had shot. He praised the majesty of its antlers. He told of how, imitating the ritual attributed to Native Americans, he drank a sip of the blood of the first deer he killed. And he spoke with great appreciation for properly cooked venison as a veritable delicacy. Then my urban prejudice and hypocrisy became clear. I ate meat just as much as he did. The difference was that whereas I took no thought of the life of the cow or the chicken whose meat I ate, Ralph knew the animal whose life he took and appreciated the connection between his own life and that of the deer whose flesh he ate. For me, the ground beef or chicken breast was just something you buy at the store. For Ralph, the venison was no mere commodity. It was a fellow creature.

Thinking about food in purely economic terms as a commodity that we produce rather than within the context of a theological understanding of God's creation, we develop not only a disordered view of food but also a disordered view of ourselves. Instead of living within the limits of nature, we trust our own creative power of technology to live beyond the limits of our creaturely finitude. Our technology has allowed us to so control and manipulate our environment that we have come to think of it as something of our creation rather than God's. So supremely confident are we that the solution to any problem lies in new technology that we have not until recently begun to consider living within the limits of nature. By asking the farmers and the land to produce more food for an ever-expanding population, we have sought to produce more than is sustainable for the land. As Wendell Berry explains, "We have bought unconditionally the economists' line that competition and innovation would solve all problems and that we would finally accomplish a technological end-run around biological reality and the human condition." Even as the rich fool in Jesus's parable sought security in his barns with their stockpiles of surplus grain, we seek our security not trusting in the gifts of God's providence, but in the power of our technology to satisfy our ever-expanding appetite for more of everything.

To pray for our "daily bread" is to confess that we, the children of Adam's race, are creatures of the soil. The image in Genesis of God's fashioning Adam from the dust of the earth is a poetic depiction of human nature. We are material, as well as spiritual, beings. The very substance of our bodies is taken from the earth. And in time the matter of our being returns to the earth to become life-giving food for other creatures. The petition for our daily bread is a petition of humility. The word *humility* comes from the Latin word *humus* (which is also the root of the adjective *humanus*, "human"), meaning "earth" or "soil." To be humble literally means "to be close to the ground," hence metaphorically it means "to be lowly." The Lord's Prayer challenges us to be humble in a more literal sense. For in confessing our need for bread from the grain of the field we remind ourselves that as human beings we are creatures of *humus*, the soil. In other words, we are material beings who exist in an organic relationship with the rest of creation. Instead of living disconnected from the earth, we must see our lives as part of a larger whole. When we are conscious of our dependence upon the land and the people who cultivate the land, we realize that our welfare is inescapably tied to the welfare of the lives—human, plant, animal, and soil—on which we are dependent. As they thrive, we thrive. As they suffer, we eventually suffer as well. The petition for "daily bread" teaches us the humility proper to creatures. Jesus reminds us of our absolute dependence upon God by putting in our mouths the words of a beggar: "Give us bread." Our life is truly not our own. We are beggars before God. The "bread" for which we pray is a gift of our Father who created us and is sustained by the resources of the earth that our Father entrusts to our care.

Spirit and Body United

Confessing that we are creatures of the soil united with the rest of the material universe has profound implications for rightly understanding who we are and our relationship with God. It is to confess first and foremost that we are part of God's material creation. To put it another way, we are embodied creatures composed of flesh and bone as well as soul. Our bodies are part of who we are. Being born of the Spirit at baptism does not mean that we cease to be material beings with material needs. Now this may seem self-evident and so not even worth mentioning, but in the history of the Church it has not always been a given.

In the late first and second centuries, when the Church was but three or four generations old, there was a sect of Christians who called themselves Gnostics, or "the knowing ones." Although the Gnostics were a minority, they had enclaves spread throughout the Mediterranean world. They called themselves Gnostics because they believed that they had received secret knowledge—*gnostic* comes from the Greek word *gnōsis*, meaning "knowledge"—that gave them salvation. The secret, saving knowledge, which they claimed that Christ had revealed, was that the material world is not real; salvation, therefore, is deliverance from the illusion of the material world. This idea came from two sources. First, they misinterpreted Paul's statement that Christians no longer live according to the "flesh" but according to the "Spirit." They thought that "flesh" referred not to "sin," as Paul meant it, but to the body itself. Second, they viewed the body as the source of evil. After all, the Gnostics said, the body is the cause of unholy passions (such as lust) that lead us into temptation, of pain (such as a migraine headache or the agony of arthritis or bone cancer) that prevents us from doing what we really want to do, and of ignorance and deception (such as when our eyes tell us there is water on the road in front of us on a blistering hot day).

Believing that the body and all matter is the cause of evil in the world, they asked the obvious question, "Why would a God who is all-good, all-wise, and all-powerful create the material world that is the cause of evil?" Their answer: such a God would not create the material world. In their view, reality was divided between the realm of light, which was eternal, immaterial, and real, and the material realm of darkness, which was the source of ignorance and sin. This material world, they concluded, was created by a being called the Demiurge, whom we might think of as being like a powerful but ignorant angel who believed he was god. This Demiurge or creator god, they claimed, was the god whom the Jews worshipped. The God whom Jesus revealed was not the creator god at all but the true God, who is purely spiritual as are his true followers, the Gnostics. They even went so far as to say that Jesus was not really a person of flesh and bone, a person like us. Rather, the Son simply *appeared* to have the form of a man; in fact he was without a body, like a ghost or hologram. Since they believed that the material world was the source of evil or unreal, they either shunned all things material, including sex and marriage, or they felt free to do with the body whatever they wanted, since the body was of no real importance. Ultimately, they did not believe in the resurrection of our material bodies. Instead, they claimed that death would free them from the prison of the material body and their spirits would ascend to God.

The Alternative to Gnostic Spirituality

The Gnostics' view of the material world and God was roundly condemned by the bishops of the Catholic Church (what the pagan philosopher and critic Celsus called the "Great Church") as contrary to the essential teachings of the apostles. First, whereas the Gnostics denied the unity of the Old and the New Testaments, the Church insisted that the God revealed in the Old Testament and the God revealed in Jesus and recounted in the New Testament are the same God. Second, whereas the Gnostics saw the material world as the cause of evil, the Church confessed the claim of Genesis that God created the world and that the world he created was good. Third, whereas the Gnostics denied that there was a real incarnation or resurrection, the Church proclaimed what Paul said was of "first importance": that Christ was raised bodily from the dead and that in the fullness of time would return to raise our bodies, transforming them into the glory of his resurrected body (1 Cor 15:3–8, 42–44). What the Church understood that the Gnostics missed was that God is Lord of all things, including the material world that seems now to be broken, defective, and the source of pain. Salvation is not liberation from the material world. Rather, it is the renewal and transformation of the material creation (cf. Rom 8:18–23). The promise of the gospel is that the God who created the world and who in Christ liberated us from sin and death will heal his creation, which has been corrupted and broken by our sin. Christ's resurrection from the dead marks the beginning of a new creation. For when the decay and suffering associated with death come to an end, then God's creation will be brought to perfection. As Paul says, our bodies that are buried in corruption shall be raised incorruptible; the mortal shall become immortal (cf. 1 Cor 15:42–44, 53–55). Creation and redemption are not contraries, as the Gnostics taught. On the contrary, God's work of redemption described in Revelation is nothing other than the purification and completion of the work God began in Genesis.

This right understanding of redemption changes the way we think of the body. To begin with, instead of thinking as the Gnostics did that the body and all of material creation is the source of evil and therefore something that prevents us from knowing God, we believe that God uses the material world to turn our minds to him. Commenting on the creation story in Genesis 1, Gregory of Nyssa asks why God made humanity last among all creatures. His answer: God is like a good host who sees to it that the feast is ready before his guests arrive so that all might be ready for their pleasure. In the goodness and pleasantness of creation, in that which we experience through our senses, we apprehend the goodness of God. Then our minds are raised above the material world to meditate upon the invisible God who is its cause. All of creation, when rightly understood and rightly ordered, reflects the wisdom, power, and goodness of God.

This is not to suggest that we have a Pollyannaish view of creation. Ours is not what Harvard paleontologist Stephen J. Gould derided as the "all things bright and beautiful" argument for God's existence. Our judgment of the goodness of creation is not based on a willful blindness to the realities of "nature red in tooth and claw." The majestic mountains that turn our minds heavenward were fashioned by the violent process of surging magma and plate tectonic shifts that produced earthquakes and tsunamis. If God is the creator of all things, then God must be the creator of the malaria-carrying mosquito as well as the monarch butterfly. Life is sustained by death. The speed and agility of the cheetah that are a wonder to behold are creative adaptations that allow the cat to thrive by preying on the old, the young, and the weak. Ours is the God of the cheetah as well as the God of the baby gazelle on which the cheetah feeds. These realities we cannot ignore. Rather, we are forced to recognize that God's immeasurable goodness and infinite power cannot be sentimentalized or domesticated. They force us to take seriously the intricacy and complexity of God's creative wisdom. "My thoughts are not your thoughts and my ways are not your ways," God declares through the prophet Isaiah (Isa 55:8). So we marvel at the wonders of the material world and the inscrutable wisdom of God whose hand is behind it all. Scripture itself contains sayings and stories that don't easily mesh with the kingdom Jesus preached. Our right response is not to turn a blind eye to such passages but to stop and probe more deeply the mystery that God has revealed. So too the natural world—what medieval theologians called the "book of creation"—is full of paradoxes to which we, as people who follow the one who is the Truth, cannot turn a blind eye. Rather, we let the paradoxes become the occasion for deeper reflection on the wonder of God's providence that assures the good not of individual creatures alone but of the whole of creation.

The Gnostics either would not pray for "daily bread" or would give those words an entirely immaterial or spiritual meaning. But when we pray for "our daily bread" we are affirming that it is our heavenly Father, not some ignorant and deluded demiurge, who created our bodies. We rely on our Father for the food needed to sustain those bodies. But even more we realize that the gift of material creation itself is God's tool for revealing his goodness to us, that our minds might be drawn back to him. Thus we ask for bread in order that as creatures of the soil we might be conscious that the divine hands that formed our bodies continue to care for them. When we confess our need for daily bread, we train ourselves to think of food as a gift of God, an expression of God's grace. The psalmist declares, "O *taste* and see that the Lord is good" (Ps 34:8). In the sweetness of the ripe watermelon, we apprehend with our senses God's gracious providence. From the fiber and nutrients of a head of spinach, our bodies derive the strength and energy that God intended for us. In faith, we not only taste the sweetness of the fruit or feel the health provided by the spinach; we are conscious of God's daily provision for our needs. The Lord's Prayer raises our vision above the categories of biology and economics to see "our daily bread" theologically as a gift that reveals our Father's patient and enduring love for his creatures.

Our Daily Bread

In chapter 6, we examined the significance of Jesus's instructing his disciples to pray not with the singular "me" or "my" but with the plural "us" and "our." The reason, we saw, was that we do not pray as individuals but collectively, as the body of Christ. For we are not his only children and our relationship with God is always as members of the community of believers united by one and the same Spirit. The significance of the first person plural "our" has implications for how we understand the petition for "our daily bread."

Once, when I was lecturing to a group of Episcopal pastors in South Sudan, one of them raised his hand and asked, "Why do you still need to pray for daily bread?" He went on to explain the reason for his question: "We live in a world of the haves and the have-nots. You are from among the haves. You have plenty of food. So why do you need to ask God for food?" I was initially taken aback by the question. It was one of those telling questions that allowed me to see myself through another person's eyes. Though I would hardly be counted as wealthy by American standards, that is just how this South Sudanese pastor saw me. And given the standard of living of the people to whom he ministers, I was more like the rich man and they like Lazarus. In that awkward moment, however, the significance of "our" jumped out at me. I still need to pray "give us this day our daily bread" because Jesus commands me to pray that *all of us* receive our daily bread. The petition for "daily bread" is not for *my* bread, but for *ours*. When I pray for "*our* daily bread," I am conscious of our common need for bread. I am reminded that as a son of our heavenly Father I have a familial obligation to see to it that my sisters and brothers, and all who I hope will become my brothers and sisters, will receive the healthy food and clean water, safe housing and respectable clothing necessary for our life together in the kingdom. It is a confession of my moral duty to do for "the least of these my brothers" as I would for Christ himself. As John Wesley said, "There is no holiness except social holiness." To live into the holiness proper to the life of a son or daughter of our holy heavenly Father, we must seek to do justice for those who are hungry not just for bread but for all the material goods essential to flourish as a child of God.

Conclusion

By teaching us to pray for our daily bread, Jesus teaches us not to create in our minds a dichotomy between the spiritual and the material, the heavenly and the earthly, the private and the public. In confessing our creaturely need for the food that gives strength to the body, we see ourselves rightly as part of creation—a creation that is both spiritual and material. We glimpse the unity of God's creative purpose that the world should be a holy place where we encounter God's grace that provides for our needs, both of the body and of the soul. By using the word *bread*, which has such a range of meanings in Scripture—from the manna in the wilderness, to the body of Christ, to the word of God, to food on the kitchen table—Jesus teaches us to see our whole lives as interconnected with all the creation that is an expression of God's provision. Ours is not a Gnostic universe divided between the material and the immaterial, the realm of darkness and the realm of light. The Spirit sanctifies the mundane and the earthly contains heaven. This is what it means to think about even the most ordinary dimensions of life through the lens of the Incarnation. The eternal Word of God is present to us in flesh and blood, in bread and wine. The Holy Spirit may speak to us in the gravelly voice of an octogenarian standing at the bus stop or from the careworn face of an Iraq War veteran breaking bread with us at a Wednesday night dinner. When we confess our need for daily bread for the body and speak with confidence of faith that our heavenly Father will provide, we learn to see God's life-giving providence in all things. Then our prayer is training us, preparing us for life in Christ's eschatological kingdom in which, as Paul declares, we shall experience God as our "all in all."

10

Restoring the Covenant

"Forgive us our trespasses as we forgive those who trespass against us."

THE ISRAELITES HAD BEEN traversing Sinai's wilderness for decades, waiting for God to allow them to enter the promised land. Their sojourn in the desert gave little evidence that they had learned anything from the forty-year "time out" for their disobedience and disbelief. There were repeated breaches of their covenant with God, the covenant made on the lower slopes of Sinai where God adopted the children of Israel as his children, the covenant that was to order their life as a nation dwelling in the promised land. While they plodded through the land of Moab before crossing the Jordan River into Canaan, God, ever patient with his people, instructed Moses to renew the covenant with his children. He reminded them of the compact between God and them, of their mutual promises and obligations: "The LORD will again take delight in prospering you . . . if you obey the voice of the LORD, to keep his commandments . . . if you turn to the LORD your God with all your heart and with all your soul" (Deut 30:9–10). Then Moses summed up the significance of this covenant. He laid out the bottom line: "I have set before you life and death, blessing and curse; therefore choose life, that you may live and your descendants may live, loving the LORD your God, obeying his voice and clinging to him" (Deut 30:19–20).

"Choose life." This was Moses's parting advice to the people he had led. It is the same exhortation Jesus gave when he announced, "I came that you might have life and have it abundantly." This is the life he offers in the new covenant—the covenant that is the foundation of the Lord's Prayer.

To pray the Lord's Prayer is to choose life. It is to confess the new covenant inaugurated in baptism and to turn our hearts to God who gives us the Spirit, who is the seal of our covenant, adopting us as his children. In the petition for "daily bread" we choose life by confessing our need for the food without which life would go out of our bodies. We also confess our dependence upon God to provide that life-giving bread from the earth and the life-giving bread of heaven—Christ's own body.

Yet Jesus knows his people. We, like the Israelites in Moab, do not always choose life. We stand at the fork on the highway through the desert and we choose death. Perhaps not intentionally. But in turning from the Lord, in failing to cleave to the one who is life, in trusting our own wisdom and desires, we cut ourselves off from God and thus from life. For sin is a betrayal of our pledge and promise, a breaking of the covenant. Like an astronaut whose lifeline to his ship has been severed and who helplessly floats off into the lifeless vacuum of space, in sin we are loosed from our godly moorings and so we drift off into the darkness waiting for death, which, apart from God, is inescapable. But to us, as to the Israelites, God holds out the offer of the covenant again and says, "Choose life." So when Jesus instructs us to pray "forgive us our trespasses," he is telling us to repent of our sin and reclaim the new covenant with our Father who is the fount of life.

Back to the Font

When we pray "forgive us our trespasses," we are returning to the baptismal font. This is where we were brought as infants or were led as adults by grace. Either way, we came to the baptismal font to receive the forgiveness of sin, to be "washed in the blood of the lamb," thus becoming members of the new covenant in Christ's blood. Here we were adopted into the family of God called Israel, and here we began our journey, like the ancient Israelites, to the promised land. We map out the route of this spiritual journey by telling a story, a story theologians call "salvation history." From creation and the fall through the cross and resurrection to Pentecost and the prophecies of the Christ's return, it is the story of God's calling his creatures into relationship with him as his children. The centerpiece of the story is summed up in Paul's words, "God was reconciling the world to himself through Christ" (2 Cor 5:19). In baptism we enter into a covenant of reconciliation with God, and in praying "Forgive us our trespasses" we confess that covenant. It is a covenant with God inaugurated by the atoning death of Jesus. Before discussing the atoning work of Christ, we need to say something about the trespasses for which we need forgiveness and atonement.

Debts or Trespasses?

My father once co-officiated at a funeral with a Presbyterian pastor. All went well until they got to the Lord's Prayer, which my father was to lead. My father, in deference to his Presbyterian colleague, who he knew would say "debts" rather than "trespasses," said, "And forgive us our debts as we forgive our debtors." But his Presbyterian counterpart, knowing my Methodist father was accustomed to saying "trespasses," prayed, "And forgive us our trespasses as we forgive those who trespass against us." A moment of liturgical confusion motivated by ecumenical good will. Why the confusion? Which is it—"debts" or "trespasses"?

The Greek word is *opheilēmata*, meaning "things that are owed" or "debts." So why do some traditions pray "and forgive us our trespasses" instead of "debts"? The confusion can be put at Jesus's feet. At the end of the prayer, Jesus comments on the petition about forgiveness. There, however, he speaks not of forgiving "debts" but rather "trespasses" or "transgressions" (*paraptōmata*). In either case, the terms are synonyms for "sin." For example, there are two ways we are in debt to God. The first is a natural debt—what we might call a "debt of gratitude." In previous generations (think of a Charles Dickens novel), people who were done a great kindness would have said to their benefactor, "I'm in your debt." In the case of God, this natural debt is the obligation of obedience that comes from our relationship with our Creator. God created the world for us to inhabit and gave us life. We owe all things that we love to him. So that means using all things as he wills for our happiness. This is not the debt Jesus has in mind. He is not teaching us to ask to be freed from our obligation to obey and serve our Father. That is what the prodigal son did when he asked for his inheritance and then left home. It would be the dissolving of our covenant with God, like a divorce in which the man and woman renounce their covenantal obligations to each other as husband and wife. This is not the debt we ask to be forgiven.

There is a second debt that comes as a result of sin. It is the debt that results when we fail to pay what we owe. In the United Methodist Church, all candidates for ordination as clergy are asked a series of questions that John Wesley asked his preachers; among them is this question concerning finances: "Are you in debt so as to embarrass yourself?" At this point everyone laughs, knowing how sizable their debts are from school loans accumulated over four years of college and three years of seminary. This is not what Wesley had in mind—or could even have imagined. The embarrassing debt that Wesley was thinking of was debt that comes from living extravagantly, beyond one's means, and failing to pay one's creditors—which, in eighteenth-century England, was a crime that could result in imprisonment. So too, our failure to fulfill our covenantal obligations to God—the obligations of obedience to the commandments, especially the commandment to love God with all our heart, soul, mind, and strength, and our neighbor as ourselves—is a debt to God.

St. Anselm put it this way: it is appropriate that we honor that which is good and excellent. Since God is supremely good and excellent, then we owe God our highest honor. Sin, doing our own will, is not only a failure to honor God; it is an insult to God and it is degrading to humanity. Thus sin brings shame and a debt of honor.

This debt of sin can also be thought of as a trespass. For to trespass means to violate the property boundaries. It is to cross a line one should not cross, to go where one has no business going. In establishing moral and spiritual obligations and expectations, the covenant sets the boundaries or parameters of our relationship with God. But sin transgresses those boundaries. We cross a line, the line between Creator and creature, when we presume to be our own lord and master, living according to our own will and wisdom rather than our Creator's. Whether we think of sin as a debt or as a trespass, the effect is the same. Our sin, like that of the Israelites grumbling in the wilderness against the very God who had delivered them from Egypt, is a failure to put our lives in God's hands and a failure to love God in the way he requires. It is a breach of the covenant, a breaking of the bonds of friendship that leaves us alienated and estranged from God. If the breach is to be mended and the severed bonds of friendship repaired, there must be atonement. Whether we speak of debts or trespasses, we are confessing that we have not given God the unconditional love and obedience that is his due. We are confessing our infidelity, which has created a rupture in our covenant with God. That covenant can be restored only if we are reconciled to God. This reconciliation is called by theologians "atonement."

An Atoning Bath

The word *atonement* is an Anglo-Saxon word, meaning "at-one-ment" or "to be made one." In Christian parlance, the atonement refers to Christ's work of reconciling sinful humanity with God. By his incarnation, death, and resurrection Christ overcomes the rupture in our relationship with God and with one another that we may again be one family under the fatherhood of God. Christian baptism is an outward and visible sign that we are reconciled to God through the forgiveness of our sins. Originally, John the Baptist used the waters of the Jordan River as a sign of the repentance of all who came to him to be baptized. For Christians, the water of the baptismal font is the sign of the cleansing of Christ's atoning sacrifice.

Early in the Fourth Gospel, John the Baptist is instructing his disciples and he sees Jesus walking not far off. John breaks off his teaching and, pointing at Jesus, tells his disciples, "Look there. That is the lamb of God who takes away the sins of the world." To John's Jewish disciples, the description of Jesus as "the lamb of God" would have triggered two important associations. First, they would have thought of the story of the exodus. They would have remembered how Moses instructed the Israelites to mark the doorposts and lintels of their houses with the blood of a lamb so that, when the angel of death swept through the land of Egypt, killing the firstborn son of every Egyptian household, the angel would pass over the houses of the Israelites, sparing them from death. So too, John was saying, Jesus is the one whose blood will save us from death.

Second, John's disciples would have made an association with Yom Kippur, the Day of Atonement. On that day the high priest entered the innermost section of the temple, the Holy of Holies. This housed the ark of the covenant, which contained the stone tablets of the covenant God gave to Moses and was understood to be the earthly throne of God. Before the ark, the high priest would sacrifice a spotless lamb for the forgiveness of sins. He would throw the lamb's blood upon the lid of the ark, called the "mercy seat." The lamb was a sacrifice—an offering unto the Lord of that which is good and pure and holy as a sign of repentance and submission to God. The high priest was understood to be standing in for Moses. Even as Moses had ratified the covenant between God and the Israelites by sprinkling the blood on the altar and upon the people, so now the high priest was reestablishing the covenant between God and Israel through the lamb's blood poured upon the altar that is the mercy seat. Even as the blood of the lamb sacrificed on Yom Kippur gained forgiveness for the sins of Israel, now John was saying, Jesus is the lamb of God whose blood takes away the sins not of Israel alone but of the whole world.

John's Gospel makes Jesus's identity as the lamb of God who delivers humanity from sin and death clear in its narrative of Jesus's passion. In Matthew, Mark, and Luke, Jesus's last supper is a celebration of the Passover meal, after which he is arrested and, on the following day, put to death. In John, however, there is no Passover meal. Rather, "before the feast of the Passover" (John 13:1) Jesus has supper with his disciples, during which he washes their feet as a dramatic parable to begin his farewell sermon. As in the other gospels, after the supper Jesus goes out to pray in a garden. There he is betrayed by Judas, arrested by the temple guards, tried by the high priest, and then sentenced to death by the Roman governor, Pontius Pilate. But John makes a point of telling his readers that Jesus is crucified and dies on the day of Preparation (John 19:31), the very time when the lambs were being slaughtered in preparation for the Passover meal. Thus, in John's Gospel, Jesus is the sacrificial lamb whose death upon the cross is a sacrifice for the forgiveness of sins, and by the sacrifice of his blood we are delivered from the sentence of death.

The book of Revelation, also called the Apocalypse of John, illustrates the relationship between Christ's atoning death on the cross and the new life begun in baptism with one of its typically unusual visions of God's kingdom on earth at the end of time. In chapter 7, John has a vision of God the Father seated upon his throne. Standing to the right hand of the throne is the risen Christ, depicted as a lamb whose body bears the marks of having been slain. Before the throne of God and the Lamb stand an innumerable multitude from all the nations of the earth; they are clothed in white robes, and like the throng that welcomed Jesus into Jerusalem on Palm Sunday, they wave palm branches and shout out, "Salvation belongs to our God who sits upon the throne, and to the Lamb!" Then one of the elders standing around the throne questions John:

> "Who are these, clothed in white robes, and whence have they come?" I said to him, "Sir, you know." And he said to me, "These are they who have come out of the great tribulation; *they have washed their robes and made them white in the blood of the Lamb.* Therefore are they before the throne of God, and serve him day and night within his temple; and he who sits upon the throne will shelter them with his presence." (Rev 7:13–15)

The multitude in white robes standing before the throne and worshipping God and the Lamb are all people from every time and place who are Jesus's disciples. Their white robes are the robes that in many ancient services of baptism were used to clothe the newly baptized immediately after they rose from the water of the baptismal font. White is a symbol of purity and heavenly glory. What is peculiar, however, is the source of the robes' whiteness: the blood of the lamb in which they have been washed. This is strange indeed. We think that something that has been washed in blood would come out a crimson red. But these robes are white as if washed in bleach.

Here John has mixed two images to say something profound about what it means to be a disciple. Revelation unites the image of being washed in the water of baptism with the spiritual cleansing that comes by the forgiveness of sin through Christ's death upon the cross. In other words, the water of baptism is a sign that we are cleansed of sin by being "washed in the blood of the lamb." When we accept the forgiveness of sin God offers us through Christ's death on the cross, the stain of sin has been removed; the debt has been forgiven. God has removed the trespass that alienated us from him and prevented us from living in fellowship with God. This is atonement. It is about being made clean, and it is God himself who cleanses and purifies us.

In our society, which now has hand sanitizer pumps in bathrooms just in case good old soap and water are not enough, it is easy for us to take getting clean for granted. In first-century Judea, however, being clean was not so easy. The Torah required that one's hands and pots and plates be cleansed. If someone suffered from a contagious disease, such as the skin disease leprosy, they were cut off from society. Lepers were required to announce their presence by crying out, "Unclean, unclean," as they walked the street. For the time, these were understandable precautionary measures. But being unclean prevented the lepers from joining together with other Jews in table fellowship. It made them strangers and outcasts.

Sin has the same effect in our lives. We are all guilty of having made a promise, with the best of intentions about getting it done, but not fulfilling it, either because of some legitimate reason or some lame excuse. In that situation, we feel bad every time we see the person to whom we made the unfulfilled promise; nagged by feelings of guilt, we go out of our way to avoid him. We feel "unclean" in the sense that we have a profound sense that things are not right.

So it is when we have broken our covenantal promises to God. The guilt can be soul-crushing. "Being cut off from God" is no metaphor; it is a painful existential state. We feel as if there is a dividing wall between God and us. Hear the good news: God in Christ has torn down the dividing wall. In baptism he has called us: "Come and get clean." When God forgives the sin that separates us from him and from one another, he unites us to himself in a new covenant. When we pray "forgive us our trespasses," we are claiming the promise of forgiveness offered to us in the new covenant that rests upon Christ's atoning death.

Why the Cross?

When thinking about the atonement, one question always comes up. What is the relationship between Christ's work of reconciliation and his crucifixion? Did the Father will Jesus's *death*? Did God need Jesus's death to set the cosmic scales of justice in balance or to appease his wrath? There are no facile answers to questions about the cross. One important and helpful way of thinking about the meaning of Christ's atoning death comes from Paul's depiction of Jesus as the second Adam. He introduces this comparison between Adam and Jesus in his letter to the Church at Rome: "As sin came into the world through one man [Adam] and death through sin . . . then as one man's trespass led to the condemnation for all men, so one man's act of righteousness leads to acquittal and life for all men" (Rom 5:12, 18). Paul's argument is this: Adam's trespass was his disobedience. In eating the forbidden fruit, Adam and Eve refused to submit to God's lordship and to trust his word to direct them in the way of happiness. The result was that he and his children were subject to Adam's punishment, death. All who have followed Adam, even if their sins were not the same sin as Adam's (Rom 5:14), have faced the same penalty. For all our sins are but imitations of Adam's archetypal disobedience. But if all humanity could be led into sin by the sin of one man, Adam, could they not also, Paul reasons, be led to righteousness by the righteousness of one man, Jesus? The act of righteousness Paul has in mind is Christ's perfect obedience: "For as by one man's disobedience many were made sinners, so by one man's obedience many will be made righteous" (Rom 5:19). Obedience—humble submission to the will and authority of God: this is the righteousness that God wanted from humanity from the beginning.

In Paul's mind, Jesus reconciled humanity, restoring us to a right relationship with God because he gave the Father what Adam did not, his perfect love and obedience. The reconciling work of Christ occurred not just on the cross but also throughout the entirety of Jesus's earthly life. For his whole life was one of fidelity manifest in his obedience to the Father. The cross is the climax of that life of voluntary submission, for the cross was the culmination and consequence of his obedience to the Father. Because Jesus was faithful to his mission of proclaiming the kingdom of God, his uncompromising declaration of the kingdom challenged the priests and leaders of Israel who misused their authority and offended the self-righteous by exposing their hypocrisy. Such faithfulness to God inevitably gets one killed. But by submitting to the cross, Christ demonstrated supreme fidelity: unconditionally surrendering to the Father the very life the Father gave him. In that, Christ revealed the perfect love the Father desires of his children. We are to love God not because he blesses us but for his own sake, simply because he is God. As Anselm put it, by his perfect obedience, in doing the Father's will, even to the point of giving up what he did not owe, his own life, Jesus showed such honor to God that he satisfied our debt of honor. Moreover, in showing God the honor that is his due, Christ restored to us the dignity proper to human beings, who were made to enjoy praising the goodness of the God who made us and called us friends.

Easter is the sign of our reconciliation with God. At Easter, the Father revealed his approval of Christ's faithfulness by raising Jesus from the dead and restoring to him the very life he laid down. Paul's insight was that in Jesus's perfect faithfulness to God, finally one of Adam's race got it right. Finally one of us gave to God the devotion he asked of us. In Jesus, God and man are reconciled because in Jesus's relationship with God we see true righteousness. On the cross, we see that the righteousness of Jesus is the just submission and obedience to the Father. In the resurrection we see the righteousness of God, who is merciful to sinful humanity, giving them new life and the promise of resurrection. When we come to the font to be baptized, we are reconciled to God when in faith we accept both his sacrifice for the forgiveness of our sins and his obedience unto death as the pattern of righteousness that with the aid of the Spirit we will strive to imitate.

Precisely because Christ accomplished our reconciliation with God by his obedience unto death, we should never speak those words "forgive us our trespasses" too quickly or glibly. We cannot take forgiveness for granted. The forgiveness for which we ask came at a dear price; the work of reconciliation and of the restoration of justice is never easy. The forces of injustice always resist, often violently. Jesus confronted sin. In opposing it even with the sacrifice of his own life, Jesus fulfilled John's prophecy and became the lamb of God who takes away the sins of the world. So when we pray, "forgive us our trespasses," we are invoking Christ's sacrifice for the forgiveness of sins. Because his sacrifice was the sacrifice of obedience, Jesus showed us what unconditional obedience to God is. Since his obedience becomes the foundation for a new relationship between God and his people, when we pray "forgive us," we are promising God that we will strive to live into this new covenant based on the example of Christ's perfect obedience. Implicitly, therefore, we are offering him our very lives as a sacrifice in union with Christ's sacrifice.

A Prodigal Love

Our petition "forgive us our trespasses" expresses contrition for our sin and confidence in the forgiveness of our sin through Jesus's atoning death. It rests upon our faith in God's love of us—our trust that the Father hears our contrition and out of a deep love forgives the debt that we cannot repay.

Because Jesus is fully God and fully man, he reveals perfect humanity—as in his obedience unto death—but he also reveals the heart of the Father. The richness of the gospel narratives lies in the interplay between what Jesus teaches and what Jesus does. He tells simple parables and then makes the stories come to life in his actions. He is the woman in the parable of the lost coin who sweeps the house from top to bottom, looking for the one lost silver coin. He is the good shepherd who leaves the ninety-nine sheep to go in search of the single lost sheep. This was his ministry, the mission on which the Father sent him: to save the lost sheep of the house of Israel. Yet Jesus adds to these two parables a third parable, arguably his most skillfully crafted, that speaks not of his mission to find and bring back the lost, but rather of the ones who are lost and the Father who waits for their return.

Reams of paper have been devoted to discussing what to call this parable in Luke 15 about a younger son who leaves his father to go off into the distant country and the father who welcomes him home. Some have called it the the Parable of the Lost Son to parallel the titles of the preceding stories, the Parable of the Lost Sheep and the Parable of the Lost Coin. Others have said that Jesus is really contrasting the younger brother and the elder brother, who was faithful to his father while his younger brother was off living a decadent life and who now resents the celebration being given in honor of this unfaithful wastrel. So they say it should be called the

Parable of the Two Sons. Still others say that the father and his relationship with both sons is the centerpiece, so the story should rightly be titled the Parable of the Loving Father. The number of possible titles is as great as the layers of meaning Jesus packs into this parable consisting of a mere twenty-one verses. Despite all these alternative titles, however, it remains most commonly called the Parable of the Prodigal Son. Yet I would argue that this title, though I use it all the time, is somewhat misleading. For the true prodigal in the story is not the younger son, but the father.

The word *prodigal* is not common in contemporary parlance. It is a Victorian expression that has fallen out of use. No one ever uses it except when referring to this parable. Its primary meaning, of course, is "extravagant or wasteful," often with the connotation of riotous and immoral living. In fact, this connotation comes from its association with the conduct of the younger son. Yet I came to a new appreciation of the word *prodigal* some years ago while reading an old translation of Aristotle's *Nicomachean Ethics*. Aristotle described virtue as "the golden mean." It is the mean or middle point between the extremes. For instance, courage is the mean between the extreme of cowardice, on the one hand, and the extreme of recklessness, on the other. When he comes to the subject of giving away money, he calls the mean "liberality," or as we might say today, "philanthropy." Liberality requires knowing how much one can afford to give away and giving it only to those who are worthy of our help. Philanthropy, he says, is the mean between the extreme of deficiency, "miserliness"—that is, not giving away any money but hoarding it—and the extreme of excess, "prodigality." By "prodigality" Aristotle means spending or giving away more money than you can afford such that you fall into debt and lose your financial security. But it also means giving money and gifts to the *wrong sort of people.* Aristotle then goes into great detail to illustrate the difference between those who are worthy of our gifts and those who are unworthy.

The unworthy are those who lack good character. They are wastrels and profligates who misuse the gift of charity. They lie and deceive in order to persuade you to write them a check. I once heard an interview with a woman who, after winning the lottery, received a letter from her next-door neighbor pleading for help with paying taxes on the house. After some investigation, she discovered that there were no back taxes due. It was all a con. The unworthy are those to whom the prodigal gives but who give nothing back in return. They are moochers who feign friendship in order to be invited to dinners or the lake house on the weekend. They are users who seek friendship not because they genuinely like you but because they believe they can gain advancement or a promotion at work.

By Aristotle's standards, the younger son in Jesus's parable is unworthy. He had broken the bonds of family affection and abdicated his familial duties. In taking his inheritance prematurely, he treated his father as if he were dead and of no consequence. Far from investing his inheritance wisely and living moderately, the boy led a lifestyle of excess and debauchery that left him penniless, friendless, and homeless. He "came to himself" only after having hit rock bottom while he was slopping the hogs and coveting the pods in their food trough. But even when he conjured up the plan to go home and offer himself as a servant to his father, the son was not thinking of his father but of filling his empty belly: "How many of my father's hired servants have bread enough and some to spare, but I perish here with hunger!" (Luke 15:17).

While in seminary I heard a dramatic reading of this story that offered a different interpretation of the son's motives than that suggested in most traditional readings. In this reading, the son was not truly contrite. Rather, out of hunger and desperation he works out a plan to restore himself to his father's good graces: "I will arise and go to my father, and I will say to him, 'Father, I have sinned against heaven and before you; I am no longer worthy to be called your son; treat me as one of your hired servants'" (Luke 15:18). He carefully chooses his words—just the right mixture of piety and self-abasement. It is a con, one he rehearses to himself all the way home. But when the son sees his father—the father whom he'd abandoned but who now is running to embrace him—he cannot pull off the con. In the face of his father's undisguised joy and relief, the son is reduced to humility and a true sense of his unworthiness. Artifice gives way to genuine contrition. He speaks the speech he had rehearsed, but now he speaks the words from his heart. How does the father respond? He calls for the best robe, shoes for his feet, and a ring for his hand. These are not the clothes of a servant, but of a child. They are the signs of the sonship that the boy had rejected but that the father now has restored.

By Aristotle's standard, the father in the parable is not virtuous. He is not being liberal but prodigal. The robe, the ring, the fatted calf—these are gifts of which the son is unworthy. This self-absorbed brat who has been hurtful and disrespectful to his father, who has squandered his half of the family estate in licentious and self-centered living, and who now returns without any good works to warrant the father's renewed trust—this unworthy son is now being restored to his place of privilege, to equal standing with the older brother, who has remained faithful the whole time. This is not liberality. It is foolishness and injustice. But Jesus justifies the father's prodigal love: "My son who was dead is alive again" (Luke 15:32). To be sure, the son must prove the sincerity of his contrition and his desire to live as a child in his father's house, under his father's authority. But now, in coming home to his father, the son has chosen life.

The motto of South Carolina, *Dum spiro spero*—often loosely translated as "where there's life, there's hope"—goes to the heart of the issue. By choosing life with his father, the younger son has renewed his hope of growing into the man his father wants him to be. But it is a hope that begins with the unmerited love of the father, who offers him a new start on life and a second chance. With this parable, Jesus reveals the character of the Father who sent him to seek and save the lost. By Aristotle's perfectly reasonable standards, this parable should be called the Parable of the Prodigal Father. For in baptism, God claims us as his children, placing on us the robe of adoption, a robe washed white in the blood of the lamb. He does this not because we are worthy of his lavish, pardoning grace but because he wants to give us the life of the saints, and with it the hope that as we abide in his house, submit to his authority, and feast at his table, we will grow into the image of our holy Father.

When we pray, "forgive us our trespasses," we are choosing life in God. For we are confessing not only our sins, which would cut us off from God, but also our total dependence upon the Father's prodigal love for us. It is not a love that forgives us and restores us to right relationship with him because we have done something to merit forgiveness. It is a love that forgives, and forgives, and forgives, in order that we may renew our hope of eternal life in the new covenant.

11

"That They May Be One": Forgiveness and Reconciliation

"... as we forgive those who trespass against us"

"FORGIVE US . . . AS we also forgive": these are the most unsettling words in the Lord's Prayer. If we were fully conscious of their meaning and implication, they would not slip off our tongues so easily. God's covenants with Israel in Scripture list reciprocal obligations. There are promises and conditions. It is never a unilateral promise, but always quid pro quo. To childless Abraham, God made the promise, "I will make of you a great nation and will bless you and make your name great so that you are a blessing." On Abraham he placed the condition, "Go from your country, your kindred, and your father's house to the land that I will show you." At Sinai, God made the promise, "You shall be my treasured possession out of all the people." God also set this condition: "if you obey my voice and keep my covenant" (Exod 19:5). So too with the new covenant, Christ gives the promise of forgiveness. But the promise carries a condition. When we pray as Jesus taught us, "Forgive us our trespasses *as we also forgive* those who trespass against us," we are asking God to forgive us in the same way that we forgive others. God will show us mercy if we likewise show others mercy. The deeply troubling implication is that if we do not forgive those who have sinned against us, neither shall God forgive us our sins. What is profoundly troubling is that if we are really honest with ourselves, we know how hard it can be to forgive others as fully as we want God to forgive us.

But as children of the new covenant in Christ's blood, we are under the obligation to forgive.

A Parable of Forgiveness

At the end of the Lord's Prayer, Jesus goes back and offers a commentary on only one part of the prayer. He passes over all the other petitions, as if they were self-explanatory, and returns to the petition for forgiveness. He wants to make absolutely clear that his disciples understand the meaning and implication of this petition. "For if you forgive men their trespasses, your heavenly Father also will forgive you; but if you do not forgive men their trespasses, neither will your Father forgive your trespasses" (Matt 6:14–15). The obligation to forgive clearly was a stumbling point for the disciples. Sometime later, Peter returns to the subject and presses Jesus to see just how serious he was: "Lord, how often shall my brother sin against me and I forgive him? As many as seven times?" Peter must have thought about the question carefully before asking it, for he poses the scenario in which forgiveness is hardest: the *repeated* violation of our trust. Except for most egregious sins, we usually can forgive once or twice fairly easily. What is hard is when the one we have forgiven seems to take it lightly, wrongs us for a second (or third) time, then comes to us again seeking forgiveness. The alcoholic who has promised a hundred times to stop drinking and to get help but now, after an ugly episode, makes the same old promise—and this time he really means it—if only you won't leave him. Or the coworker at the office who comes to you the Monday after a church retreat to apologize for talking behind your back and to ask forgiveness, but who by Thursday is back to her old ways. Yet Jesus tells Peter that forgiveness is more than simply giving a second chance: "I do not say [forgive] seven times, but seven times seven." Then, in his typical fashion, Jesus explains the reason for our obligation to forgive—again and again, if necessary—with a parable of two servants who were in debt. It is worth hearing as a whole.

> "The kingdom of heaven may be compared to a king who wished to settle accounts with his servants. When he began the reckoning, one was brought to him who owed him ten thousand talents; and as he could not pay, his lord ordered him to be sold, with his wife and children and all that he had, and payment to be made. So the servant fell on his knees, imploring him, 'Lord, have patience with me, and I will pay you everything.' And out of pity for him the

lord of that servant released him and forgave him the debt. But that same servant, as he went out, came upon one of his fellow servants who owed him a hundred denarii; and seizing him by the throat he said, 'Pay what you owe.' So his fellow servant fell down and besought him, 'Have patience with me, and I will pay you.' He refused and went and put him in prison till he should pay the debt. When his fellow servants saw what had taken place, they were greatly distressed, and they went and reported to their lord all that had taken place. Then his lord summoned him and said to him, 'You wicked servant! I forgave you all that debt because you besought me; and should not you have had mercy on your fellow servant, as I had mercy on you?' And in anger his lord delivered him to the jailers, till he should pay all his debt. So also my heavenly Father will do to every one of you, if you do not forgive your brother from your heart." (Matt 18:23–35)

Jesus the master teacher often used hyperbole to create vivid and memorable images to get his point across to his disciples. This parable is a classic example. Jesus is contrasting the master's willingness to forgive his servant's debt of ten thousand talents with that same servant's refusal even to be patient with a fellow servant who owed one hundred denarii. In the first century, a talent of silver (roughly eighty-five lbs.) corresponded to half a year's wages for a common laborer, whereas a denarius was a common laborer's daily wage. So when Jesus says that the first servant owed his master ten thousand talents, that is hyperbole. Ten thousand talents is a sum so great it is intelligible only to the federal government. It is a sum so immense that it would take the servant five thousand years to pay off. It is a sum so vast as to be laughable were it not so tragic. Because the master knows the debt is beyond the servant's power to pay, he forgives the debt.

Now the second servant, too, is in debt. A hundred denarii is about three months' wages; it is no small sum he owes the first servant. One can imagine Jesus's audience empathizing with the first servant. To be out of pocket three months' income is no trivial matter to day laborers. Jesus knows this too. It adds to the realism of his message. Being his follower comes with a cost. Forgiving can be costly, for to forgive others is often to renounce a serious grievance or claim we have against the other person. But in comparison with the first servant's debt to his master, the one hundred denarii is minuscule. Relieved from the burden of his onerous obligation to his master, the first servant should have been equally merciful to his fellow servant. He should have passed on his good fortune. Yet his refusal to show an ounce of patience to a fellow servant, let alone the same forgiveness the master showed him, rightly earns him the wrath of his master: "You wicked servant! I forgave you all that debt because you besought me; and should not you have had mercy on our fellow servant, as I had on you?"

Our debt to God—the God who gave us life, who gives us all the goods of life we love and enjoy, who sustains us even when we turn away, and who is patient when we fail to give him the profound gratitude we owe—is infinitely greater than any debt another person could owe us. Therefore, if God forgives us our vastly greater debt, who are we not to show the same forgiveness to others? When Jesus teaches us to pray, "forgive us . . . as we forgive," he is calling us to acknowledge that God's forgiveness of us is contingent upon our forgiveness of others: "So also my heavenly Father will do to every one of you, if you do not forgive your brother from your heart." Here Jesus is suggesting a variation of the Golden Rule, "Do unto others as you would have them do unto you": do unto others as you would have God do unto you, because God will do unto us as we do unto others. When we pray, "Father, forgive us our debts, even as we forgive our debtors," we are confessing that our heavenly Father, who has called us to share in his holiness, expects us to forgive others as he forgives us. This is what Jesus meant when he told his disciples, "A new commandment I give you, that you love one another as I have loved you" (John 13:34). God's prodigal love is manifest in his boundless patience and forgiveness. This forgiving love is the very standard God has set for his children, and it is a standard he expects all who claim his name to live up to.

When I was in graduate school, my roommate and I shared an upstairs apartment in a rambling, old Victorian house that was converted into a combination office building and dance studio. One summer my roommate wanted to go home. So, to cover his share of the rent, he sublet his room to a fellow who had recently immigrated to the United States from Haiti and was making ends meet by teaching music lessons at a local school. Although conscientious and hard-working, he could not always make ends meet. When my roommate returned at the end of the summer, the fellow did not have enough money to pay him the rent he owed. "That's okay. Pay me when you have it," my roommate told him. But he never had it. The debt was becoming something of an embarrassment. There were phone calls with awkward apologies for not having the money, always accompanied by promises that it would be paid. After a couple of months, my roommate said, "Don't worry about it. You don't have to pay me anything. I got to stay at home rent free, so I'm not really out anything." The rent money was not insubstantial. But in the proverbial grand scheme of things, the debt was small and the joy of getting to be home with family for the summer was worth far more than the rent that he forgave.

When we pray, "Forgive us our debts, as we forgive our debtors," those words must be framed in our mind by Jesus's parable of the debtors. We are confessing that neither we as debtors to God nor our brother as a debtor to us can know peace under the alienating burden of the debt of sin. So we confess our desire to be free from that debt of sin. We, therefore, renounce our brother's debt to us, giving him the same freedom and peace that we seek from God.

Forgive and Forget?

One of the most common comments people make about forgiving others, especially when what they must forgive is a horrific injury, either physical or psychological, is this: "I can forgive, but I can't forget." This comment is important because it forces us to think more fully about what it means to forgive someone. When we say we can't forget, we mean that our relationship with the other person is forever changed by his action. The mother of a dear friend told me the reason she had divorced her first husband. He left her to have a fling with another woman. Eventually, he came to himself and, realizing his foolishness, went back to his wife and asked her to take him back. Without any hint of bitterness, she told me, "I will always love him. But I could not trust him." So she could not take him back. While the pain may subside, the memory of that betrayal cannot be erased and so will forever be the association that defines the way she thinks about her ex-husband. He is a man who cannot be trusted.

If God's forgiveness of us is the example of how Jesus expects his disciples to forgive, we must ask, "How does God forgive? Does he also forget?" The psalmists often use the language of "remembering" to describe how God deals with our sin. In Psalm 79, the author pleads with God, "Do not remember against us the iniquities of our forefathers; let thy compassion come speedily to meet us, for we are brought low. Help us, O God, for the glory of thy name; deliver us, and forgive our sins, for thy name's sake" (Ps 79:8–9). What does it mean to ask God not to remember sins? How, after all, can an omniscient God not remember the past? In Psalm 103, the psalmist gives us the answer. With great confidence, he declares, "God does not deal with us according to our sins, nor requite us according to our iniquities. For as the heavens are high above the earth, so great is the steadfast love toward those who fear him; as far as the east is from the west, so far does he remove our transgressions from us" (Ps 103:10–12). God does not suffer from a weakness of memory; he does not experience bouts of amnesia. Rather, God does not hold our sins against us. God does not keep our past sins forever hanging over our heads. They are not a weapon, a means of power or manipulation. For God's love, not our sins, defines our relationship with God.

Aristotle said that we are what we do. It is not our intentions or our motives or our circumstances that define who we are. It is, he said, our actions. But as Christians, our primary identity is given us in baptism. It is an identity defined by the relationship with God that began when, in the waters of baptism, our sins were sacramentally washed away and we were born anew as children of God. That covenantal relationship takes priority over everything. Even as a parent's love for her child is prior to and independent of anything the child may do, so God's love for his children is not conditioned by how righteous we are. When the psalmist says, "as far as the east is from the west, so far does he remove our transgressions," he means that God does not let these sins determine our relationship with him. They do not define who we are in his sight.

If this is the character of God's forgiveness, what is the character of the forgiveness God expects of us? God does not expect us literally to forget the past any more than he does. To forget thus, if even possible, would be to live in a state of denial. Such a life would lack truthfulness and honesty. I recently saw a set of four horrific pictures with captions that a former student posted on Facebook. The first picture was of the World Trade Center in flames; the caption read, "Never forget." The second picture was of Jewish children in a concentration camp; the caption read, "Never forget." The third picture was of the genocide in Rwanda; the caption read, "Never forget." The final picture was of the grotesquely scarred back of an ex-slave; the caption read, "Get over it." Whether the caption on the final picture accurately characterizes the attitudes of white Americans toward the memory of slavery and our racial history and toward the way black Americans think about the antebellum South and Jim Crow is up for discussion. But it does speak to how selective our memory can be. Some things cannot be forgotten. We erect monuments and designate certain locations as historic sites. We call them "memorials" because their purpose is to prevent us from forgetting either acts of great virtue or deeds of unspeakable atrocity. For it is in remembering that we are both inspired and humbled. In remembering the past, we find models to emulate and models that remind us of the depths to which all people, however supposedly enlightened and cultivated, are capable of sinking. We can never forget, nor should we. But forgiveness changes what we do with those memories.

When we pray, "Forgive us . . . as we forgive," we confess that we must forgive because God has forgiven us. Our recollection of the trespasses of others against us is laid alongside the memory of our own sins. It is therefore a confession of our mutual need for forgiveness. Martin Luther King Jr., during the civil rights movement, spoke of our "mutual indebtedness." He exhorted blacks and whites to remember that we are indebted to one another for raising up this nation. But we are also to call to mind our "mutual indebtedness" before God. Neither blacks nor whites stand upon an absolute moral high ground, but all are servants indebted to God. Such a confession forges solidarity between the trespasser and the trespassed; for apart from God's grace, both stand under condemnation before the justice of God.

There is a second way forgiveness changes what we do with our memories. When we forgive we imitate God's forgiveness of us. As God removes our transgressions "as far as the east is from the west," so do we. In practical terms that means we do not brood over the memories of the trespasses against us. We do not revisit those memories over and over as if picking at a scab. Dwelling on those memories only dredges up the hurt. Emotionally, that represents living in the past, allowing the hurt and injustice of the past to define our present relationship with the one who hurt us. Even as God "removes our transgressions" in the sense that he does not allow our past sins to define our present relationship, so too we "remove" the trespasses by not allowing them to set the terms for our relationships now. In forgiving, therefore, we surrender all claim to those memories; they have receded into the nonexistence of the past. Such memories no longer can be a weapon we use against our trespasser. When we pray the Lord's Prayer, we confess and promise that we will not continue to hold past sins over the trespasser's head for the rest of his life. If we have forgiven someone, we cannot, in the midst of a heated conversation, throw back in their face the reminder of some grievance from a month ago, or a year ago, or five (or even fifteen) years ago. In that sense, the image of forgiving a debt is appropriate. When a debt is forgiven, we renounce our claim to be repaid. We cannot come back at some future point and demand our money. That debt no longer exists. A clean slate exists between us and the debtor. The clause "as we forgive our debtors" is a declaration of that clean slate. The memory and even the pain of the debt may remain, but we have renounced our claim against our sister. Only then can we seek the grace that can heal broken relationships and ease the pain of their memories.

The Purpose of Forgiving

There is nothing uniquely Christian about forgiveness. It is virtually a universal among religious traditions. Indeed, it is not unique to religion. The value of forgiveness is acknowledged and extolled by believers and atheists alike. But there is something distinctive about the character of the forgiveness that Jesus taught—an objective that sets it apart from the forgiveness lauded by the world. In secular society, the focus of forgiveness is on the one who has been wronged; she forgives those who have wronged her so that she might be happy. Forgiving is about letting go—letting go of the hurt, the anger, the indignation, which when held onto brood and fester in the mind and eventually turn us into bitter, resentful, unhappy people. Learning to forgive is a survival skill, a strategy of self-preservation. In other words, we forgive not for the sake of the one who sinned against us but for our own psychological wellbeing. This account of the therapeutic value of forgiveness is absolutely right. Unless we can forgive, the hatred toward those who wronged us will consume our soul and diminish the quality of our life. But this is not the primary reason we who are children of God are called to forgive.

Christian forgiveness is different because it has a different end or purpose. We forgive not for our own sake but for God's. We forgive to fulfill the goal of the new covenant that binds us to our heavenly Father. The new covenant eliminated the ethnic division between Jews and Gentiles, opening the promise of God's grace to all who confess and follow Christ in faith. As Paul tells his Gentile hearers, "once you were strangers to the covenants of promise, having no hope and [being] without God in the world. But now in Christ you who once were far off have been brought near in the blood of Christ . . . who has made us both one, and has broken down the dividing wall of hostility . . . that he might create in himself one new man in place of two" (Eph 2:12–15). Even as the goal of the new covenant was to reconcile Jew and Gentile, thus making them into one people in Christ, so too we who are children of that covenant are called to a ministry of reconciliation. This is the goal of forgiveness. We forgive in order to be reconciled to one another. This is decidedly harder than the forgiveness advocated by the world. Therapeutic forgiveness is hard because it calls for us to change how we think, or more often don't think, about the person who has injured us. Reconciliation is more demanding because it seeks to change both trespasser and trespassed. It is not just about creating a *modus vivendi*—a tepid coexistence—between the estranged parties. It seeks to renew the warmth of fellowship within the bonds of peace.

In his second letter to the Christian community at Corinth, Paul explains how Christ's atoning death changes the way we view one another in a way that reconciles those who are estranged by debts and trespasses:

> From now on, therefore, we regard no one from a human point of view; even though we once regarded Christ from a human point of view, we regard him thus no longer. Therefore, if any one is in Christ, he is a new creation; the old has passed away, behold, the new has come. All this is from God, who through Christ reconciled us to himself and gave us the ministry of reconciliation; that is, in Christ God was reconciling the world to himself, not counting their trespasses against them, and entrusting to us the message of reconciliation. So we are ambassadors for Christ, God making his appeal through us. We beseech you on behalf of Christ, be reconciled to God. For our sake he made him to be sin who knew no sin, so that in him we might become the righteousness of God. (2 Cor 5:16–21)

Reconciliation is possible because Christ changes the way we see one another. When Paul says he no longer regards anyone from a "human point of view"—the way he had once viewed Jesus himself—he is referring to the hostility, rivalry, and division characteristic of sin. What is the alternative to seeing others from a human point of view? It is to see them from a divine point of view, from God's perspective. How? Obviously, we cannot get in God's mind and see through God's eyes, so to speak. But God's Spirit does get into our mind and does cast the light of God's wisdom on our perceptions and judgments of the world. The wisdom of God lies in the cross. The alternative to regarding one another from a human point of view is to see each other through the lens of the cross.

On the cross we see Jesus, the God-man, crucified. Because Jesus is fully God, we see the depths of the Father's love for his creatures. We realize that God is not just a father who patiently waits for the prodigal to come home. God is also the Good Shepherd who goes in search of the lost sheep, even enduring the cross to do so. Because Jesus is also fully human, he is one of us. But he is not only our brother. He is, as Paul says, the new Adam, the progenitor of a new humanity. The first Adam is a figure of fallen humanity alienated from God because of sin. As Augustine put it, we all are that first man because we have failed to pay our natural debt of grateful obedience. We have failed to render to God what we owe him. Jesus is the new Adam because he did what the first Adam did not do; he rendered to God the highest honor that is his due by being perfectly obedient. Because he was obedient, even to the point of offering to God what he did not owe—his very life—his faithful obedience reconciled Adam's race to God. We, therefore, are no longer Adam's race, but Christ's. Because Christ Jesus paid the debt of sin that stood as a barrier between God and us, he has reconciled us to God. We are no longer estranged from God by our ingratitude and self-will. As people reconciled to God, Paul realized, we are a new people, a "new creation." "If anyone is in Christ, there is a new creation"—not a creation characterized by sin but a creation reconciled and restored to God. When we pray, "Forgive us . . . as we forgive," we see the world through the lens of the cross. We see others and ourselves not as the trespasser and the trespassed against, but as Christ's new creation, a people reconciled to God. In order for the new creation that Christ inaugurated by his death and resurrection to be complete, we must be reconciled to one another.

As people who in faith are reconciled to God, we have been commissioned to carry out Christ's ministry of reconciliation. We often hear people say that since Christ ascended to the Father, we are the hands and feet of Christ, meaning that we are the instruments Christ uses to continue his work on earth. Our works of service are Christ's "hands" that feed the hungry, comfort the lonely, heal the diseased, and clothe the poor. Paul would say that we are Christ's hands and feet when, in forgiving, we carry on Christ's mission of reconciliation. When we forgive, we bear witness to God's reconciling love. In forgiving others' trespasses and seeking forgiveness for our trespasses, we remove the barriers of alienation, suspicion, and resentment that trespasses create between individuals, between factions within the Church, and between communities. As we remove those barriers, we make steps toward the unity Jesus prayed for in his priestly prayer for the Church: "Holy Father, keep them in thy name . . . that they may be one even as we are one" (John 17:11). Therefore, when we pray, "Forgive us . . . as we forgive," we are imitating not one but two of Jesus's prayers. In praying for forgiveness, we are confessing that as God's children, called to bear the holiness of his name, we are also called to work for a unity within the family of God that reflects the unity of the Holy Trinity.

Such unity is possible because of the Holy Spirit. The Spirit animates the community of believers to be the body of Christ by pouring the love of God into our hearts—a love that does not hold on to offense or resentment but forgives in order that the joy of peace and the bonds of fellowship (*koinōnia*) may be restored. Thus, our *koinōnia* mirrors the fellowship of the Trinity. As Augustine observed, the Holy Spirit is the divine love the Father and the Son have for each other that forms the Trinity. John makes the connection between the work of the Holy Spirit and the forgiveness of sins in his account of Jesus's giving the Spirit. Appearing to the disciples, who were hiding in a locked upper room, still fearful that as their master was put to death they might be next, Jesus allays their fears with the word *Peace* and, breathing on them, says, "Receive the Holy Spirit." Then he immediately begins instructing them on their ministry of reconciliation: "If you forgive the sins of any, they are forgiven; if you retain the sins of any, they are retained." In other words, by linking the giving of the Spirit and Jesus's words about forgiveness, John is making the point that the Spirit uses us as instruments of reconciliation. It is a reconciliation that comes from the pardoning of sin but also from confronting one another with the hard reality that unless we forgive, God will not forgive but will retain our sins.

If the petition "Forgive us our trespasses as we forgive those who trespass against us" expresses a genuine desire for forgiveness, it is more than simply a promise not to hold our sister's debts against her. It is a petition for peace—not simply the peace that comes from the end of hostilities but the peace that comes when we are reconciled. It is the peace that comes only when things are made right between us. It is the peace of fellowship—the very fellowship that will exist when at the resurrection we are called from east and west, north and south, to feast together in Christ's kingdom. For without the peace of reconciliation, breaking bread with our debtors in the kingdom of heaven would be an eternal hell.

Confrontation and Reconciliation

What makes the ministry of reconciliation so hard is that it is not achieved unilaterally. Yes, we forgive our brother's trespass against us regardless of whether he desires forgiveness or even recognizes that he has done anything that needs to be forgiven. If forgiveness is not just about making us feel better but about restoring the bonds of fellowship, then our prayer "Forgive us . . . as we forgive" must be accompanied by *confrontation*. To be sure, there are those small, accidental trespasses that we simply forgive without comment. But in the case of either major trespasses that have been the cause of profound hurt or small but repeated trespasses that have the effect of a thousand tiny paper cuts, we must confront our sister. If we are at fault, we seek her out to ask her forgiveness and, if possible, to make things right through restitution. But if it is our sister whose actions have hurt us psychologically, materially, or spiritually, we also must confront her and tell her what she has done. If we seek reconciliation and peace, how we confront her matters. Christian confrontation cannot be confrontational, that is, in a manner that puts our sister on the defensive. Our confrontation must be forthright but gracious, conveying our good will and our desire to heal the wound. It may be that she does not know she has done anything and is grateful for your telling her. Or she may not get it, remaining oblivious or even indifferent to the hurt she is causing. Obviously, such confrontation is not easy. If we have been at fault, it requires the courage to make ourselves vulnerable to the anger and retaliation of those against whom we've trespassed. Likewise, when we are the injured party, courage is required to reveal the emotional or physical wounds that others have inflicted upon us.

Courage is also necessary to face the possibility that our overture of good may be completely rebuffed and even turned against us. A friend told the story that at a family gathering with his in-laws a heated conversation took place between various members of his wife's family and him. When he got home from the trip, he felt bad about the argument. Both sides had trespassed, but he felt bad for the part he had played. So he wrote an e-mail to his in-laws in which he apologized. Instead of receiving his overture in the spirit of reconciliation, they saw it as a sign of weakness or an admission that he, and he alone, was in the wrong. They smelled blood in the water and renewed their attack. As in this case, confrontation can backfire. But unless there is confrontation—a time to speak the truth in love—then you and your sister can never come to a mutual understanding. For without a meeting of minds and hearts, there can be no true unity or fellowship.

We can never force reconciliation on others. As people who pray for forgiveness, for ourselves and for others, and seek reconciliation, sometimes we act in ways that create a space for the Spirit's reconciling grace to soften hardened hearts and prepare the way for healing the bond of fellowship. One Christmas some years ago, the phone rang. It was a man who had been a longtime member of my church. Something was weighing heavily on his conscience. He told me a story that I had already heard from a teenager in the church. The teenager was a sixteen-year-old girl who had known this man since she was a child. They had been buddies. She'd run to greet him whenever she saw him at Wednesday night dinners. And he'd bring her little gifts every now and then. But earlier that fall she had been elected as youth representative to the Administrative Council. During the course of a debate in the council, the man stood to speak in opposition to a proposal. When he sat down, the teenaged girl stood to speak. In a respectful and civil tone she challenged the point that her old friend had just made. In the end, the vote was taken and his side lost. The next Sunday the girl was in the narthex waiting to go to her pew when she saw this man come in. Unselfconsciously she went over to greet him. But instead of returning the greeting, the man said, through gritted teeth, "I'm not speaking to you." And he walked right passed her. The girl was shocked and confused and deeply hurt. Subsequently, whenever she saw him at church she was wary and would give the old gentleman a wide berth to pass. But the Sunday before Christmas a guest preacher had spoken on the reconciling love of God that overcomes the resentments and fears that divide us. The girl was so convicted that God calls us to share in the work of reconciliation begun in the manger at Bethlehem that she could not celebrate Christmas without being reconciled to her friend. So after the service she caught him on his way out the door and, touching his arm gently, smiled and with every bit of good will said genuinely, "Merry Christmas." For a split second, the man was taken by surprise, but then, almost as if he had been hoping for such a moment, he looked her in the eyes and replied humbly and gratefully, "God bless you, child." This was the confession he called to share that Christmas morning. He and the girl were not "buddies" as they had been years before. Their relationship had changed, but they were bound to each other anew by that gesture of reconciliation. Years later, the girl, now a young woman, discerned a call to the ministry. When she had to apply to her local church for financial assistance as Duke and all seminaries ask students to do, the older man stepped forward as one of her most vocal and generous supporters.

This is what it means to live into the new creation as sisters and brothers reconciled to God and to each other. When we pray, "Forgive us our debts as we forgive our debtors," we are confessing our faith in both the reconciling love of God manifest in Christ's death on the cross and the power of Christ's Spirit to pour that love into our hearts, that we may confront and overcome the sins and the festering memory of those sins that divide us, and so come to live as one family under the fatherhood of God.

12

Confessing Our Vulnerability

"Lead us not into temptation, but deliver us from evil."

THIS FINAL PETITION, AT first hearing, is one of Jesus's most enigmatic and troubling sayings. What does it mean that we should ask God not to "lead us into temptation"? Is God the source of temptation and thus the one who causes us to stumble and even fall to our ruin? Is God guilty of spiritual entrapment? We might seek a solution in the Greek words used in the New Testament. Perhaps "lead" is just an archaic translation. Perhaps the Greek word means something else that does not implicate God. Alas, no such luck. In fact, the Greek is even more problematic, for the word *eispherō* is better translated "carry into." It is the same word used by the New Testament authors when the friends of the paralytic "carry" him on a stretcher to Jesus to be healed. It might have the sense of "take" or "bring," as when an older generation of Southerners would have asked, "Will you carry me to the store?" "Do not bring us to temptation" is hardly less problematic; the petition seems to imply that God has some degree of responsibility for our temptations.

Temptation or Test?

The place to begin our search for the solution is not with the verb "lead" but with its object, "temptation" (*peirasmos*). The Greek word *peirasmos* is related to *peiratēs*, from which we get the English word *pirates*, and it can mean "temptation." But it can also mean "test," as when in Exodus the Israelites "put God to the test," that is, forced his hand to make him prove himself. *Peirasmos* can also mean "trial" or "hardship," as when Acts 20:19 says that during Paul's ministry in Ephesus he served the Lord with humility, with tears, and by enduring trials (*peirasmon*). Obviously, Paul did not serve God by setting spiritual snares for the people of Ephesus. The difference in translating *peirasmos* as "temptation" as opposed to "test" or "trial" is no mere semantic difference. It is a critical distinction that allows us to understand what it means to be a child of our heavenly Father led by Christ's Spirit.

A temptation and a test have markedly different goals. The ultimate aim of the Tempter is to cause us to fall. Temptation's goal is to cause us to assent to what we at some level know to be contrary to God's will, such that we turn from God and become lost. The aim of a test, on the other hand, is quite the opposite. Far from seeking someone's downfall, the goal of a test or trial is to challenge one in order to make one stronger. As a seminary teacher, I give tests. Contrary to what some of my students may think on the eve of the final exam, my object is not to cause anyone to fail and have to leave school. My goal is to prepare them for the demanding work of ministry by requiring them to acquire not only mastery of a certain important subject, but also, and perhaps even more importantly, the intellectual skills and the moral habits necessary for a life of studying and proclaiming the word of God. Without the intellectual skills of interpreting and explaining the Church's sacred texts, there will be no message to proclaim. Without the moral habits of self-discipline and patience, one cannot listen for the Spirit and so discern what to preach. These skills and habits are the fruits of the months of studying for the final exam. The process is unavoidably demanding and so may feel like a trial. It puts a student's determination and commitment to following her call to the test. When she comes through what may feel like an ordeal, her resolve is stronger and her knowledge greater and she is better prepared for the work of ministry.

Our Father does not tempt his children. His goal is not that we should stumble and fall but that we should be sanctified. So God does not lead us into temptation on the road to perdition. But he does put us through tests in order to purify our will, strengthen our devotion, and prepare us to face the world's temptations by teaching us to rely upon the grace of his Spirit. This is what the Father did to his own Son. In Luke's narrative of Jesus's birth and childhood, the gospel repeatedly comments on the boy's progress into manhood and toward the work of the Messiah: "And Jesus increased in wisdom and in stature, and in favor with God and man" (cf. Luke 2:40, 52).

Immediately after his baptism, when the Father has declared his pleasure in his Son and anointed him with the Spirit, Luke writes, "And Jesus, full of the Holy Spirit, returned from the Jordan, and was led by the Spirit for forty days in the wilderness, tempted by the devil" (Luke 4:1). God led him into the wilderness so that he could confront and overcome the temptations that awaited him in his public ministry. What the devil intended as Jesus's downfall, the Father intended as preparation for the temptations he would face: those that attend tremendous power, public adulation, and a desire to win the hearts and minds of the people. Had he used his power for self-serving purposes or sought political power or pandered to the people's expectations of the Messiah, he could not have been the Messiah his Father sent him to be. In his divinity, Christ's will was one with the Father's, but his humanity had to grow into holiness by being trained in the virtues of faithfulness and obedience necessary for his mission by confronting these temptations. Jesus could not have submitted to the burden of the cross had he not been able to resist these lesser temptations. Jesus's sojourn in the wilderness and the temptations he faced there—God's boot camp for the Messiah—made him into the man God called to deliver his people. The test that Adam faced and failed in the garden of Paradise, the second Adam faced and overcame in the wilderness, that he might regain for us the paradise Adam lost (Rom 5:18–19). Luke ends the wilderness narrative with a note of caution and a note of triumph: "The devil departed from him until an opportune time. And Jesus returned in the power of the Spirit of God into Galilee, and a report concerning him went out through all the surrounding country" (4:13–14). This side of paradise there will always be temptations, but out of them comes the power of God's Spirit.

What the devil uses as a temptation for our destruction and humiliation, God uses as a test for our sanctification and glorification. This is one of the lessons we must learn at the outset of our journey of faith. Ambrose was one of the most important pastors of the early Church. He was bishop of Milan in northern Italy in the late fourth century. It was the practice in Milan that adults seeking baptism would enroll for classes with the bishop that met daily, and sometimes twice a day, throughout Lent. They culminated in the "holy mysteries" of baptism and Eucharist during the Easter Vigil. The purpose of the classes, called *catechesis*, was to teach these adults about the God whom they would confess at their baptism and about the character of life they would begin as a child of God. So, where do you begin describing the Christian life? Ambrose chose Genesis, specifically the story of Abraham and Sarah. That makes sense because the Christian life is the life of faith, and, as Paul teaches, Abraham's faith is the model for all Christians. God called Abraham and Sarah to leave the land of the Chaldeans in the fertile crescent of Mesopotamia—the land of their families, the land of their youth, a land where people worshiped false gods—and follow him to a promised land where they would become parents of many nations. So too, Ambrose explained to his catechumens, God was calling them to renounce the pagan worship and the immorality of their past and begin a journey in faith following the one true God to a promised land called the kingdom of Heaven. One challenge that Ambrose faced was how to explain to his pupils Abraham and Sarah's sojourn in Egypt. After all, God did not take them directly from pagan Mesopotamia to the promised land. Rather, God led them first to Egypt. Now for Ambrose, as well as for most Jewish and Christian interpreters of Scripture, Egypt represented pagan religion and immorality. So why, Ambrose asked, would God lead Abraham and Sarah to Egypt? Why, having just led them out of the pagan world of the Chaldeans, would he bring them into the greater temptations of Egypt? Ambrose's answer to these would-be Christians was that God had called them to leave the worldly, pagan lifestyle of their past, but he had not called them out of the world. Rather, God would lead them to the kingdom by leading them into the world. Their lives would bear witness to the truth of the kingdom of God in the midst of the kingdoms of the world. To be in the world in order to be witnesses of God's love and justice to the world, they must be trained to face the temptations of the world. Abraham and Sarah's sojourn in Egypt was a time of testing. So too, Ambrose was saying, following God in faith is not about being freed from temptation. Far from coming to an end, the temptations simply come in subtler forms, such as the temptation to spiritual pride and self-righteousness. Praying "lead us not into temptation" is a confession of our need for faith to follow the God who leads us into the world with all the temptations it throws at us. It is a petition for grace to trust in the sufficiency of the Spirit's sustaining presence to empower us to overcome temptations.

Caution for the Impetuous

We pray "lead us not into temptation" not because God is the cause of temptation or because we impiously do not want to follow God where he will lead us. Rather, Jesus instructs us to offer this petition as a way of training us in humility. This humility is a necessary corrective to our intemperate bold-ness. This excessive zeal for Christ arises out of a devotion to Christ and a desire to be faithful and to prove ourselves faithful to him. We love his vision of a just kingdom and are enraptured by his promise of glory—a justice and glory more compelling than the unjust world and the uninspiring tedium of the quotidian. That is why the ever-impetuous "Sons of Thunder," James and John, asked to sit at Jesus's right hand and left hand in the kingdom. It is also why Peter boldly asserted, "Though all [the other disciples] fall away because of you, I will never fall away. . . . Even if I must die with you, I will not deny you" (Matt 26:33, 35). Instead of praising their zeal and promise of devotion, Jesus offers a word of caution. To the brothers, he says, "You do not know what you are asking. Are you able to drink the cup [i.e., the cross] that I am to drink?" (Matt 20:22). Even though Peter's boastful prom-ise proved hollow in his denial of Jesus in the courtyard of the high priest, after the resurrection Jesus explains to Peter that he would in time be called upon to fulfill his promise: "When you were young, you girded yourself and walked where you would; but when you are old, you will stretch out your hands and another will gird you and carry you where you do not wish to go." John adds in a parenthetical comment, "This he said to show by what death he was going to glorify God" (John 21:18–19).

When I was a boy, it was expected that on Sundays I would attend Sunday school and church in the morning, and in the evening return for the "snack supper" with the youth group before going to Sunday night ser-vice. This service was markedly different from the more formal 11 a.m. service. Instead of his black robe my father wore a simple dark suit. And instead of singing from the United Methodist Hymnal, we'd sing from the old Cokesbury Worship Hymnal that dated from 1938. These were not the hymns of Charles Wesley from the eighteenth century but all the "oldies but goodies" from the heyday of Methodist tent revivals and camp meet-ings in the nineteenth and early twentieth centuries. They were the hymns that the older generation in our church remembered from their youth. The idiom was that of a bygone day. The hymns spoke of "sinking deep in sin . . . sinking to rise no more" and exhorted us to "cling to the old rugged cross." Their aim was to prepare our hearts to come forward to the chancel rail during the altar call and dedicate—or rededicate—our lives to Christ. One of the hymns I associate with those Sunday evening altar calls was number 186, Earl B. Marlatt's "Are Ye Able." In a steady tempo and somber tune, the hymn imagines Jesus posing the poignant question to us his disciples,

"'Are ye able,' said the Master, / 'To be crucified with Me?' / 'Yea,' the sturdy dreamers answered, / 'To the death we follow Thee.'" Then the tempo would pick up and the tune would reach a crescendo as we sang the chorus triumphantly: "'Lord, we are able.' Our spirits are Thine. / Remold them, make us, like Thee, divine. / Thy guiding radiance above us shall be / A beacon to God, to love and loyalty." Indeed, we are not greater than our master who died on Good Friday, and so we his disciples must be willing to take up the cross. Baptism is no less than a promise to follow our Lord to death for the faith. Precisely because we are not greater than our Lord who prayed with fear and trembling in Gethsemane, we should not be eager to lay down our lives (like Peter, confidently and impetuously declaring our willingness to do so), or make any grand sacrifice, or face any temptation. There is a nobility in the faithfulness and sacrifice of the martyrs that should be honored and, if need be, imitated, but never romanticized.

One of the oldest martyr stories, dating from the middle of the second century, is the *Martyrdom of Polycarp*. This work tells the story of the arrest and execution of Polycarp, bishop of Smyrna, as an example of martyrdom that is a true imitation of Christ's death. The story begins, however, not with Polycarp but with an account of a bungled martyrdom by a young man named Quintus. The Roman governor in Smyrna had begun arresting Christians, and if they did not curse Christ and sacrifice to the emperor, then he threw them to beasts in the arena. Full of zeal for Christ and eager to prove his devotion, Quintus persuaded a group of his friends that they should hand themselves over to the governor. Boldly Quintus stepped forward to be martyred. But when the moment came and Quintus was there at the arena and heard the beasts, fear overcame his zeal, and in that very public setting before the citizens of Smyrna, he renounced Christ, making a laughingstock of himself and of the Christian faith. By contrast, Polycarp, like Jesus, did not hand himself over but waited to be arrested. With the strengthening presence of Christ, Polycarp held fast to the faith, enduring the ordeal of burning at the stake. Unlike Quintus, whose attempt to play the hero failed, Polycarp is a true martyr because his death bore witness not to his own courage but to the sustaining power of God, who gives us the ability to endure the temptations and trials that inevitably come in the world. Quintus may have been sincere, but his is the classic case of a fool rushing in where wise men fear to tread. There are enough temptations and spiritual dangers in the world without our looking for them.

The petition "lead us not into temptation" teaches us the wisdom of godly fear that is proper to humility. As with Quintus, we can be blinded by the self-confidence of our zeal to both the seductive power of temptation and to our own weakness in the face of temptation. We confuse our enthusiasm with moral fortitude, that courage given by grace that enables us to resist temptation. When we pray, "Lead us not into temptation," we are confessing how vulnerable we are to temptations and how easily we succumb to them without the aid of God's grace.

Temptation and Evil

Our journey from baptism into the kingdom of God means that we, like Jesus and Abraham, are led by the Spirit into the wilderness where we will face the temptations of the world. When we confess our vulnerability to these temptations, we set out on our daily journey with a healthy, prudent fear that rejects a Pollyannaish view in favor of a sober, realistic view of ourselves and the world in all its brokenness. Because, however, we journey in hope, trusting in God's providential care for his children, we cannot confess our weaknesses in the petition "lead us not into temptation" without immediately following with a confession of confidence in God's sufficiency as we pray, "Deliver us from evil."

In order to understand how the Father delivers his children from evil, it helps to understand from what he delivers us. We need to know something about the nature of evil itself. No doctor can prescribe the right medicine without first knowing about the disease. The problem of evil has troubled every generation of reflective Christians. One saint of the Church who was particularly bothered was Augustine. If God is the creator of all things, he pondered, is God not then the author of evil? For a period of time during his young adulthood, Augustine wandered from the Church of his mother, during which time he fell in with a religion from the east, called Manichaeism, that was widespread in North Africa. The Manicheans, like the Gnostics, held to a highly dualistic view of reality. The universe, they explained, is composed of two substances: a white substance that is good and a dark substance that is evil. Everyone's soul and body were made up of a mixture of white and dark elements. The more dark elements in one's soul, the more corrupt one was. One became spiritual by purging one's soul of the dark substance, which one did by not partaking of foods, such as meat, and not participating in actions, such as sex, that polluted the soul with their dark substance. Augustine was not content with the Manicheans' explanation for the presence of evil, but he could not come up with a better explanation—that is, until he began studying the philosophy of Plato and his disciples.

Evil, the Platonists explained, is not a substance at all. It is merely the privation or absence of good. The darkness of one's bedroom at night is not a thing or a substance that fills the room; darkness is simply the absence of light. So too, evil is not a substance; rather, some good thing becomes evil when the goodness of the thing as God made it is taken away. For example, sex as God intended it is inherently good. It becomes evil only when it is perverted by those who cheapen it in pornography or use it for mere recreation outside of marriage. The insight Augustine took from the Platonist was that evil is not stuff in the world that God created. Instead, it lies in our will—in the bad choices we make that use the good things of God's creation for some purpose contrary to God's will. Healthy bread is still good even if we eat it so intemperately that it is no longer healthy. The evil lies in our choice to eat immoderately, thus our bodies suffer from the ill effects of our imprudent choices. This was a major breakthrough for Augustine. Evil, he realized, is not something that God created; it is our creation when we pervert or misuse or love inappropriately the goodness of God's creation.

Evil has no existence on its own; it is always parasitic of the good. That is, even as a parasite cannot live except as part of its host, so too the good things of God's creation are the host and evil the parasite that exists only as a corruption of the good. This means that evil is no mere illusion; it is real. Its effects are real. In fact, the greater the good, the more devastating the consequence of its corruption. Everything that is good has a power to fulfill the good purposes that God willed. For example, a skilled orator has the power to impress ideas vividly on the minds and evoke deep emotions in the hearts of her hearers. A mediocre speaker will likely produce no great effect for good or ill in his audience. The words of a brilliant orator, like Abraham Lincoln in his second inaugural address or Martin Luther King Jr. in his "I Have a Dream" speech, not only speak to the hearts of a generation, but can shape the conscience and moral sensibilities of a nation for generations to come. But that same power of eloquent words, when on the lips of an Adolf Hitler or a Jim Jones, can seduce the mind and mobilize an entire nation of otherwise sane and moral people to madness. The goodness and power of the spoken word, when perverted by evil people for evil ends, can unleash its power with devastating consequences. So too, devotion to God, the greatest force for good in the world, can also, if perverted, become one of the greatest forces for evil. C. S. Lewis expressed the paradox: "If the Divine call does not make us better, it will make us very much worse. Of all bad men, religious bad men are the worst. Of all the created beings the wickedest is the one who originally stood in the immediate presence of God" (*Reflections on the Psalms*, 31–32).

Understanding the parasitic nature of evil gives us insight into the nature of temptation: temptation is the *deceptive* power of evil. Because evil is inseparable from what is good, it always has the *appearance* of what is good. Evil is always disguised as good and so becomes the object of our desire. When I was in high school, our chaplain, Rev. Ron McCullum, a wonderful teacher who taught the required course in Bible, told a story that made a deep impression on my adolescent theological understanding. He was in seminary in 1973 when the movie *The Exorcist* debuted. By contemporary standards of Hollywood's gory depictions of the demonic, *The Exorcist* is ho hum. But in the early 1970s, it was a shocking and disturbing story of a girl possessed by the devil and the priest who is called to perform the exorcism. In the film, young, sweet, and innocent Linda Blair is transformed into a grotesque figure whose outward form reveals the evil that lies within. Her head spins around 360 degrees; she vomits pea soup and speaks in a raspy, malevolent voice. Reverend McCullum had heard so much about the movie, and as a pastor was so often asked about it, that he felt he had to see what people were talking about. During the most shocking scenes, when this 1970s audience was gasping with fright, Rev. McCullum, much to the confusion of those sitting around him, was laughing uproariously. The reason? What a preposterous depiction of the devil and of evil. If this were the way evil manifests itself in the world, it would not be a problem. We would be able to clearly distinguish good from evil, and it would be clear that evil is undesirable. Then evil would have little power to tempt us. It is precisely because evil is camouflaged with the appearance of goodness that it is hard to tell the difference between what is truly good and what is corrupted goodness. This is the source of evil's deceptive power. This is what makes temptation so seductive.

Seeking Deliverance

Since temptation is essentially a form of deception—more often than not a form of self-deception—or of a failure to distinguish what is *really* good from what merely *appears* to be good, our petition to be delivered from the evil that tempts us to turn from God is a prayer *to see things rightly*—to see them as they are, from God's perspective. Jesus addresses the subject of temptation in his famous Parable of the Sower:

> A sower went out to sow his seed. . . . And some fell on the rock; and as it grew up, it withered away, because it had no moisture. . . . And when his disciples asked him what this parable meant, he said, "To you it has been given to know the secrets of the kingdom of God. . . . Now the parable is this: The seed is the word of God. . . . The ones on the rock are those who, when they hear the word, receive it with joy; but these have *no roots*, they believe for a while and in time of temptation [*peirasmou*] fall away. (Luke 8:5–13)

This poignant parable describes the different types of people who came to hear Jesus and how they responded to his proclamation of the kingdom. It is his explanation of why some followers bear great fruit and others none at all. The people represented by the rocky soil are particularly troubling— troubling because they are most like us. They hear Jesus gladly and respond to his preaching. His word begins to germinate in their hearts. They are on their way to becoming mature disciples. But in the heat of temptation, their faith withers and dies because, Jesus says, they have no roots. Like plants without roots going deep into the soil, drinking in life-sustaining water during periods of drought, these people have not cultivated the spiritual disciplines by which they might drink in the living water of the Spirit. Their lives stand in contrast to the blessed life of the righteous person described in Psalm 1: "His delight is in the law of the Lord, and on his law he meditates day and night. He is like a tree planted by streams of water, that yields its fruit in its season, and its leaf does not wither" (Ps 1:2–3). The disciple is righteous and fruitful because he, like the tree whose roots drink in water from the stream, abides in the word of God. He is attentive to the study of God's word and opens himself to the Spirit, who speaks to him through the words of the Scriptures. The "roots" are what John Wesley called "means of grace." These are twofold: first, *spiritual disciplines*, particularly attending to public and private worship of God, private prayer and Bible study, fasting, and the frequent and regular receiving of Holy Communion; and second, *works of mercy*, such as visiting the sick and imprisoned, providing clothing and food to the needy, and opposing social injustice. Wesley called them "means of grace" because through these disciplines and works of mercy we turn our minds from mundane preoccupations that often distract us from God and open ourselves up to receive the grace of the Spirit's presence. When we open ourselves to God's presence, we invite the Holy Spirit to reveal the Father's love and sanctify our love for him. But those who are without roots, who neither attend to the study of God's word nor open themselves to the Spirit, are ignorant of how God wills his creatures to live and become easily confused, unable to discern what is truly good and what is evil in sheep's clothing. To illustrate the point, let's turn back to Augustine.

The Platonists' solution to the problem of evil only raised another question—a question Augustine would wrestle with for the rest of his life: what causes us to make bad choices? Augustine finds one answer in the story of Adam and Eve's fall from paradise in Genesis 3. Augustine says that the original sin was not their *eating* of the fruit of the tree of knowledge of good and evil. Eating the forbidden fruit was only the outward action arising from a prior sin. They allowed themselves to be deceived by the serpent because they had become *self-complacent*. In Eden, they were accustomed to abiding in fellowship with God, who poured his light into their minds. He gave them knowledge of the good purpose of all that God made, and they took this knowledge for granted. Consequently, they became complacent, thinking that this knowledge was their own rather than a gift from God. In their complacency they did not center their minds upon God. They no longer sought the light of the Holy Spirit that was the source of wisdom. Without the Spirit's illumination, their understanding became dark. They saw the world not in the clear light of God but in the shadowy gray of twilight. With their intellect darkened, they did not see the world rightly. They did not see it through the light of God's good purposes, so they were easily confused and deceived by the serpent. Desiring to be like God is a good thing—it is what would have happened to them eventually, Augustine says, if only they had been faithful and obedient to God—but one becomes like God only by cleaving to God and living by the light of the Spirit. Because they did not cleave to God and abide in the light of the Spirit, they became forgetful of God's word and believed the serpent's lie. They allowed themselves to be suckered by a partial truth, not realizing that every lie is a partial truth, a distortion of the way things actually are. Apart from the light of the Spirit, we too do not see the world rightly and can be tempted to take moral shortcuts to achieve good ends. This is precisely how the devil tempted Jesus in the wilderness.

Augustine's idea of spiritual complacency strikes me as a helpful way to think about how we fall into sin. Most Christians do not consciously rebel against God's will. We don't wake up in the morning shaking our fist at God, yelling, "I'm going to do things my own way today, thank you very much!" Rather, sin is something we fall back into unexpectedly because we have become complacent. It happens most subtly in the paradise periods of our lives—when life has been going well. Things are okay; our guard is down. We seem to have everything in order, so we do not feel the need to cleave to God and seek his help and guidance that we did during the hard times, when it looked like we were going to lose our job due to downsizing or when our spouse was diagnosed with lymphoma. The Sunday after September 11, 2001, a neighbor said to a pastor friend, "Well, I guess you liked what you saw today," meaning the high number of people who attended services all over the country that Sunday. Much to the neighbor's confusion, my friend, unimpressed, just shrugged: "We'll see how many of them are back next week or a month from now." When life returns to normal, we fail to be mindful of our absolute dependence upon God. Without the means of grace, we become spiritually inattentive. Unintentionally and unknowingly, we drift off the trail. No longer walking in the light, we wander into the shadows. Our prayers become infrequent and our devotional life undisciplined. This is the self-complacency Augustine had in mind.

When we fail to cleave to God and open our minds to his word contained in Scripture, we have no roots to drink in the living water. If we do not abide in the company of the Spirit who speaks to us through the Scripture and sheds the light of divine wisdom upon our intellect, then we fail to see the world as it really is from God's perspective. We fall back into the old habit of thinking about our life and about the world according to the logic of the world—the way we, like Nicodemus, did before we were reborn in the Spirit. Consequently, like Nicodemus, we cannot seek the kingdom of God, nor can we understand the world according to the wisdom of God's goodness. Then we are easily deceived.

Some readers, I imagine, may understandably object that the world we live in is not a world of black and white. It is a world of shadows, and our moral dilemmas are choices between shades of gray. Even walking in the light of the Spirit, the moral choice is not always clear. More often than not, even when we earnestly desire that God's will be done, we are confused precisely because we are choosing between conflicting goods rather than between good and evil. Simple Christians, we are tempted to say, see the world in black and white; mature Christians see the world in its complexities and so are not taken in by simplistic, dualistic views of reality. Two things are worth noting. First, precisely because we live in a world of gray shadows and because we can never be quite sure how pure our motives are, we need all the more to use the means of grace to seek the Spirit's guidance in discerning our Father's will. Second, seeking our Father's kingdom is not simply about making a seemingly infinite series of the right moral choices. That is a moralistic view of Christianity that reduces the life of faith to following ethical maxims. Seeking the kingdom is primarily about living into our baptismal covenant, cleaving to God and trusting in his power and his grace working in us to accomplish his will. Indeed, the most pernicious deception is believing that it is *all up to us* to bring in the kingdom. It is to be forgetful of all God has already been doing and will continue to do to usher in his kingdom.

One of the great spiritual guides in all of Christian history is the collection of sayings of the Desert Mothers and Fathers. These sayings are vignettes describing the spiritual struggles of the monks who left Egypt's cities to live in its rugged and dry desert, either in communities or in isolation. In these stories, the monks were constantly visited by demons, who took various tempting forms that arouse certain passions or tempers. They might come as a sexually alluring woman, or as sweet food, or as an annoying sister monk, or as the impulse of self-righteousness. The senior monks, called *Abbas* ("fathers") or *Ammas* ("mothers"), teach the young monks to recognize these temptations for what they are: demons. They are deceptions and perversions intended not only to turn their minds from God, but also to make them think of themselves as base creatures cut off from God. So they name the demons: Lust, Avarice, Pride, Resentment. They are the personifications of our disordered loves and vicious habits. Then the *Abbas* and *Ammas* instruct the monks to make the sign of the cross, and at the sign of the cross the demons flee. Making the sign of the cross enables the monks to resist temptation because they remember that on the cross Christ overcame the temptations of the world and, by his obedience to the Father, reconciled Adam's race to God. Moreover, the sign of the cross is the sign of their baptism, in which they were given both forgiveness of sin and the Spirit of adoption by which they became children of God empowered with Christ's Spirit to overcome the ruler of this world who is our tempter. When we, like the monks, remember that by his death and resurrection Christ Jesus, our divine older brother, has overcome the temptations of the world and inaugurated a new creation in which we are able to walk anew in the light of his Holy Spirit, then we too are able to overcome temptations just as Jesus did.

When we pray, "Lead us not into temptation but deliver us from evil," we are confessing that God, who calls us to be his witnesses in the world, calls us, as John puts it in his Revelation, to live in Satan's shadow—the shadow of death and worldly temptation. There the greatest temptation is to think that evil and death have the final word. It is the shadowy deception telling us that we are but mortal animals, that we differ from the great white shark or Bengal tiger only in that we have bigger brains that allow us to be more destructive in pursuing our desires. It is a shadow that can make us forget our true identity—forget who our Father is and how our Brother restored us to him. So in this final petition of the Lord's Prayer we confess how vulnerable we are to daily temptations because of our inability, apart from grace, to see clearly and resist the distorted picture of reality that the world presents us. As children filled with a godly fear in the face of temptation, we confess our confidence that as our Father leads us into a world filled with temptations, he will give us his Spirit to abide with us and to illuminate our vision that we might see through the illusions and deceptions of the world. The grace of the Spirit's illuminating presence not only exposes the corrupt desires of our own hearts and the distorted picture of reality that the world presents us, but even more it reveals the Father's love manifest in signs of the kingdom all around us. This final line of the prayer is our confession that God will turn the world's temptations into tests of faith that purify and build us up to receive the inheritance among the holy children of God (cf. Acts 20:32). In the confidence of this confession, we rejoice even in the face of temptations, knowing that God will use the sufferings and trials, like the fire of a goldsmith's furnace, to purify our faith, that we may live into our holy covenant as children of our heavenly Father.

EPILOGUE

A Life of Doxology

"For Thine is kingdom, and the power, and the glory forever. Amen."

ON SEPTEMBER 14, 2001, during the National Service of Prayer and Remembrance at the National Cathedral in Washington, DC, Denyce Graves sang Albert Hay Malotte's 1935 musical setting of the Lord's Prayer. If ever there was a time when a people needed to slow down and attune their thoughts to our Lord's words, it was then. As a mezzo-soprano whose vocal range far exceeds that of most members of your local church choir, Ms. Graves lent the power of her voice to express the urgency of that hour—an urgency the spoken words by themselves could not convey. Some, I suspect, focused on the beauty of her voice. Others vicariously sang the prayer with her, using the music to raise their souls to the Father whose wisdom and comforting presence they sought.

When Ms. Graves moved from the final petition, "deliver us from evil"—particularly poignant at that moment—to the concluding doxology, "for Thine is the Kingdom and the power . . ." her voice, changing in its timbre and increasing in intensity, ascended the musical scale from C to E, rising to the soft crescendo of F, and finally to G at the prayer's climax: "and the glory forever!" At that moment the softness and the range of her voice gave the sense of transcendent worship that those final words call for. Indeed, such transcendence is precisely what we seek when giving praise to God.

This conclusion—often called "the doxology"—is not, however, part of the Lord's Prayer as it appears in either Matthew or Luke. Although the phrase "for thine is the kingdom, and the power, and the glory forever" was added in some later manuscripts—making Scripture conform to the practice of the Church—it is absent from the earliest manuscripts of Matthew that date from the fourth century. Rather, the doxology is the conclusion of the Lord's Prayer contained in an ancient Christian text known as the *Teaching of the Apostles*, or *Didache* for short. The *Didache* is a manual or "church order" that provided early Christians with instructions on worship, prayer, and discipline based on teachings attributed to Jesus and passed on by the apostles. In addition to providing the earliest form of the ritual for baptism and Eucharist, it contains teachings on prayer and fasting, including a version of the Lord's Prayer with only minor differences from the version preserved in Matthew. One of the differences is the addition of the conclusion: "for yours is the power and the glory forever" (*Didache* 8:2). There is no reference to "the kingdom." So why was the doxology added, and where did it come from?

Some scholars, such as Joachim Jeremias, have speculated that in the primitive Church, the person praying the Lord's Prayer would tack on her own petitions to form a conclusion to the prayer. Often prayers familiar to Jewish Christians concluded with a doxology. For example, the Aleinu—a commonly recited prayer in synagogue worship—ended with a doxology that began, "for yours is the kingdom." Similarly, a Jewish confession of sin concluded, "Praised be the name of his glorious Kingdom forever and ever." These doxologies echo David's benediction in 1 Chron 29:11–12: "Thine, O LORD, is the greatness and the power and the glory, and the victory and the majesty; for all that is in the heavens and in the earth is thine; thine is the kingdom, O LORD, and thou art exalted as head above all." Among the blessings over meals prescribed by the *Didache* is found the ending doxology, "to you is the glory and the power forever" (*Didache* 10.2). From this evidence, we can make an educated guess how the form of the Lord's Prayer that we say today likely came to be. Jewish Christians in the first and second centuries wanted a way to end the prayer Jesus had taught the apostles. Naturally enough they drew on the examples of synagogue prayers they were accustomed to praying. Thus they incorporated the language of "kingdom" from Jewish prayers into their own formula of "for thine is the power and the glory forever."

Regardless of the historical particulars, the doxological ending is appropriate. If the Lord's Prayer is a confession of the new covenant—a confession of the God who has claimed us as his children—then the prayer is certainly an act of praise. At the beginning of his autobiographical prayer

Confessions, Augustine says that we were made for doxology: "To praise you is the desire of man, a little piece of your creation. You stir man to take pleasure in praising you, because you have made us for yourself, and our heart is restless until it rests in you" (*Confessions* 1.1.1). When Augustine meditates on the question of why he needs to offer this confession to the God who knows him altogether, he expresses the answer in the form of a petition to God: "Accept the sacrifice of my confession offered by 'the hand of my tongue' (Prov 18:21) which you have formed and stirred up to confess your name. . . . Let my soul praise you that it may love you, and confess to you your mercies that it may praise you" (*Confessions* 5.1.1). Whether or not we know it, whether or not we believe in God, because God made us for fellowship with him, for enjoying his goodness, he made us with both a capacity to know him and a desire to praise him. Because we have the capacity for self-transcendence, the ability to imagine a universe larger than ourselves and greater than our intellect can grasp, we have an intuitive sense of a reality greater than ourselves, greater than our clan or tribe, greater than our nation, greater even than that corner of the cosmos we call our home, the Milky Way. This intuition of the greater reality is an intuition of God. It evokes wonder and speculation and inspires inquiry and study. In this way, we are hardwired with a desire for God, even if we do not know it is God whom we desire.

Because God is not a great impersonal reality, like the sun, but is the one who made us to become his children, we are also hardwired with a desire to love and to be loved. It is a desire for something so good that we find fulfillment in devoting our lives to it. We seek such a good to love in different places throughout our lives. As children we find this good in our parents' love. As adolescents, we seek it in our friends and especially in our first love. As adults, we may find it in our spouse or children or vocation. We may even seek such pleasure in devotion to sports teams or our motherland. We want to love something greater than ourselves. But we also love these people at a preconscious level because they mirror, albeit imperfectly, the goodness and love of God. Without knowing it, we love in them what we really desire from God. Yet no being other than God can satisfy that longing. So we are ever seeking the one whose goodness is worthy of our full devotion and whose love is completely satisfying.

Praise, or doxology, is how we both *express our love* for God's goodness and how we *enjoy* God's goodness. Sometimes love is expressed in performing a duty that is necessary but in which we take no delight, such as when a parent donates a kidney to her child. Sometimes love is accompanied by great delight, such as when at the end of a long Lent and an intense Maundy Thursday and Good Friday our voices break forth into heartfelt choruses of "Alleluia" on Easter morning. Love finds its fulfillment in the joy of praise. Thus God did not fashion us for praise in order to satisfy his cosmic ego; he made us for praise so that we might delight in celebrating his love for us and in loving him in return. To praise is to love, and vice versa. Our confession is both. To confess God as our Father is to declare his love for us revealed in Christ's new covenant and felt in our hearts by the unction of his Spirit. For to tell the story of God's mighty works among us through his Son and in us through his Spirit is to praise the wonders of his kingdom. In confessing his glory and power by proclaiming his kingdom, our hearts are stirred to love him. Confession brings to our thoughts a consciousness of God's goodness that inspires deeper love for God. The more we are stirred to love, the more we desire to praise and the more we delight in praising.

Sometimes, as in Ms. Graves' soaring conclusion of the Lord's Prayer, praise can have an almost *ecstatic* quality that takes us out of ourselves. It is being caught up in love for the God whom we know is infinitely greater than we are. When we come to the climax of our prayer—"for Thine is the kingdom, and the power and the glory forever"—we lose ourselves in worship. For in this final clause, the pronouns "us" and "our," ubiquitous in the previous petitions, give way to the pronoun "Thine" (or "yours"). It is doxology that takes us out of ourselves and reminds us that all we seek is the glory of our Father. It is an ecstatic, transcendent moment, especially when expressed in Malotte's music, because it is an act of surrender—surrendering our impulse for control and the desire for recognition and glory from men. Giving up the desire of the hypocritical Pharisees to be praised by men, we are content only if God is glorified. In that ecstatic desire for God's glory, our desire is, if but for a moment, truly holy. Then our righteousness surpasses that of the scribes and Pharisees.

However ecstatic our love for God may be in times of worship, the doxology at the end of the Lord's Prayer is never so otherworldly as to be separate from our life in the here and now. In confessing the Father's eternal kingship, power, and glory, we are confessing something important about life within the new covenant: our glorification of God in praise and in labor is but a reflection of God's glory in which he invites us to participate. In Jesus's high priestly prayer, on the night before his crucifixion, he entreated the Father, "The hour has come. Father, glorify the Son, that the Son may glorify Thee" (John 17:1). There is mutuality in the Father and Son's glory. Jesus was asking that the Father glorify him by revealing at the resurrection the glory that was his as the eternal Son of God. In his obedience to the Father and his triumph over sin and death, Jesus gave glory to the Father in fulfilling the Father's will of reconciling humanity to himself. Similarly, we imitate Christ our brother in ascribing to our Father the kingdom, the power, and the glory. But as children of the new covenant, we have, as joint heirs with Christ to our Father's kingdom, received the promise of our Father's glory. So we also ask the Father to give us, his children, a share in the glory of his grace that we may glorify him.

That sounds presumptuous, as if we are coveting our Father's glory. Yet Jesus promised his disciples, "Truly, truly, I say to you, he who believes in me will also do the works that I do; and *greater works* than these will he do, because I go to the Father. Whatever you ask in my name, I will do it, that the Father may be glorified in the Son; if you ask anything in my name, I will do it" (John 14:12–14). Even as the Son glorified the Father by his works, fulfilling the Father's eternal plan of salvation, so too we, who are born of water and the Spirit and have received the power to become children of God, will do greater works that glorify our adopted Father when Christ's Spirit works within us and uses us as instruments of the Father's kingdom. Indeed, this is our glory: that the Father's will is fulfilled on earth as it is in heaven. When we pray "for thine is . . . the glory" we are invoking our Father to empower us with his Spirit that we may glorify him as Christ glorified him.

While doxology is an end in itself—we never have to justify worship as if it were merely a means to some greater end—Christian praise is never kept to ourselves. It is not confined within the walls of our room where Jesus sends us to pray or of the sanctuary where God's children gather to praise our Father together. Because the praise of confession is inherently an expression of love poured into our hearts by the Holy Spirit, then our confession and praise are always *evangelistic*. Even as the Spirit placed on the apostles at Pentecost heavenly tongues of fire to confess God's mighty works in the tongues of all nations and thus make them members of the new covenant, so too our doxology is an expression of the Spirit's love in us. Such a love radiates outward, that in our praise we may be "a light unto the nations," drawing all people to our Father that they, too, may receive the power to become children of God. In this is our Father glorified.

CPSIA information can be obtained
at www.ICGtesting.com
Printed in the USA
LVHW092238200219
608278LV00001B/77/P

9 781625 647061